THE END GAME:
The REason, REsponsibility, REality & REwards of Sports

RE SPORTS
VOLUME 1

Bo Porter & Debbi Taylor

Published in Houston, Texas by SuburbanBuzz.com.
Publishing company is an imprint of SuburbanBuzz.com LLC.
www.suburbanbuzz.com

SECOND EDITION

Printed in the United States of America

ISBN: 0-9896377-7-8
ISBN-13: 978-0-9896377-7-0

DEDICATION

My sports story began in Newark, New Jersey where the majority of the playing conditions were not considered safe for children, parked cars, vehicles driving through the block or the houses in the neighborhood. At any moment a ball could go flying through a house window, or someone could get tackled on top of a car. If you lived on 14th Street in the 70's, 80's and 90's I'm sure you participated in or witnessed "Pole to Pole" football, a basketball game played on the sidewalk with a tire (used as the rim) nailed to a tree and a pick-up game of baseball in the famous church parking lot. The raw talent level in these games was comparable to the talent level at the NFL Combines, The McDonald's All-American Basketball Game and The Perfect Game MLB National Showcase.

Pole to Pole football was played in the middle of the street and the goal lines were the light poles on the sidewalk. Cars could and would drive by at any moment, at which time the game would freeze, and then continue once the cars passed. Was it safe? No! But that was the only place and space we had to play. Finding an old tire for our basketball rim was never challenging. The real challenge was finding a ladder, the nails, a hammer and a smoothly paved sidewalk! The bumpy surface made dibbling the basketball extremely difficult but it also helped improve your ability to handle the basketball. The church parking lot was our Yankee Stadium but it had one major apparent downfall that actually became the beginning of "The End Game" as it relates to my story. Let's just say home runs were not a good thing! You will read more on the significance of home runs being hit in the church parking lot in Chapter 6.

When I stop and look at my life I realize what a major role sports have played in my overall growth. But that growth would have not been possible without my childhood friends, teammates, coaches, mentors, opponents, fans and my family. My life in sports includes so many influential and impactful people that it would not only be unfair, but also impossible to name them all in this dedication. What I can say is that I've always tried to learn from every person with whom I've been blessed to share space.

So I'm dedicating *The End Game* to all those whose lives I have encountered and paths I have crossed to date and will encounter in the future as well. I am fortunate that so many people helped me along my journey and throughout this book I will share stories that will pay homage to many. I only wish that every story that has been embedded in my memory and heart could be included in written word but the pages would never end. I am forever grateful for each person that has been transformational in my life and it is my deepest appreciation in the solace of knowing that it takes a village.

Thank you. I am forever grateful to the village who has helped paved the way for me to write *The End Game*.

FOREWARD
by Debbi Taylor

"Many of life's failures are people who did not realize how close they were to success when they gave up." -- Thomas Edison

Driven. Amazing. Passionate. Generous. Brotherhood. Unselfish. These are words used by Bo Porter's friends to describe him. In this book you will gain an understanding of how hard work and dedication can lead you to achieving beyond expectations. I would describe Bo Porter as a very focused and kind man. In *The End Game* he will share extremely valuable experiences both personally and professionally so you, too, will have a better chance of living "The End Game".

The first time I met Bo Porter was back in 2007 when I was an in-game television reporter for the Washington Nationals Baseball Club and he was the third base coach for the Florida Marlins. Yet, before we even met I observed his kindness and generosity. He was always quick to share a smile or toss a baseball to a youngster in the stands at a ballgame. Since I've gotten to know Bo Porter over the years I realize what a unique individual he is. I've never met anyone so dedicated to helping others and so smart, yet sincere, in how he goes about achieving his goals every step of the way.

Bo Porter is a true example of someone working to overcome obstacles at nearly every level of life. When I traveled to his hometown of Newark, New Jersey in the spring of 2016 to attend a baseball field dedication in his name I had a chance to get an up-close and personal look at exactly what Bo Porter had to overcome to become the man he is today. I visited the neighborhood where he grew up and I met his friends and family who kept him safe from the dangers of the inner city streets. I learned how and why his inner circle worked so diligently to protect him from the crime, drugs and element on those Newark, New Jersey streets. There was something special about this person named Bo Porter. Starting from the early days as a youngster growing up in the 1970's to who he has become today, an articulate and educated entrepreneur. It has been a long journey for Bo Porter and it isn't about to end. And, what makes this journey all the better is Bo's ability to make an impact and touch lives along the way.

In Houston alone, he has the ability to impact the lives of 4,000 children daily through The Stacey and Bo Porter SELF Foundation. The idea is focusing on Sports, Education, Life skills and Faith. The youngsters come from underprivileged families where poverty has hindered their exposure to achieving higher education and development, which ultimately affects their ability to earn gainful employment and earning power. Bo Porter and his wife, Stacey, are working diligently to change the culture of these inner city children by providing them with resources to overcome that adversity.

Bo is also touching lives with his Texas Hawkeyes select baseball program that he created and still runs. Josh Jones remembers watching a man named Bo Porter spending countless hours on the Westbury field to improve his skillset. Years later he also recalls Bo introducing him to youth coaching with the Texas Hawkeyes. Jones witnessed firsthand how dedicated Bo Porter has been to his craft and how generous he is with his time as a mentor and leader. That is why Jones had great pride in congratulating Bo Porter when he was named a Special Assistant to the General Manager of the Atlanta Braves.

It was Monday, September 1, 2014 and Bo Porter had just led his team to its 59th win the day before. At the time, he was the youngest manager in Major League Baseball over the last two seasons. The win on Sunday August 31st was an eight game improvement from the previous year win total of 51 and there were still 25 games left on the schedule. That win was also against the Astros' in-state rival, the Texas Rangers. It brought the Silver Boot back to Houston for the first time since 2006.

On the first day of spring training in 2014, Bo stated his goal for the team. "Our goal in 2014 is to be the most improved team in Major League Baseball as it relates to the win-lose column," he said in front of his new players. On August 31, 2014 the Astros were eight games ahead of their win total in 2013 and in great position to accomplish this goal.

What would transpire over the next twenty-four hours is what prompted an all-out blitz to publish and release *The End Game*. Bo received the call most people never want to get from an employer. It's the type of call that can make a short twenty-minute drive seem like two hours if the person is not prepared for what follows after being fired. There are not many certainties in life, but one can assure you that most managers and head coaches can attest to the adage that they are indeed "hired to be fired". Some of our greatest and most successful managers and head coaches have been fired and some have been fired multiple times.

If you look back in sports history here are a few examples.

Bobby Cox was inducted into the Baseball Hall of Fame in 2014. He led the Braves from 1978-1981 until he was fired. Then he moved on to Canada from 1982-1985 where he was the skipper of the Toronto Blue Jays and won the AL Manager of the Year Award. After leaving Toronto he returned to the Braves from 1990-2010 and led the team to 14 straight division titles and a World Series title (Baseball HOF).

Another Hall of Famer, Yankee managerial icon Joe Torre, first managed in the big leagues with the Mets back in 1977. That year he was hired to be a player-manager. He managed the Mets for five seasons and failed to have a winning record. He was fired in the strike-shortened season of 1981. In 1982, Torre was hired to replace Bobby Cox as skipper of the Atlanta Braves. He was fired by the Braves in 1984 as the team failed to play above .500. From 1985-1990, Torre took a break from managing and spent time in the broadcast booth as a television analyst with the Angels. He also did some national network commentating for NBC and ESPN. In 1990, Torre took to the field once again, this time with the St. Louis Cardinals. It was a tough task replacing legend Whitey Herzog and Torre would be fired in 1995 (Wikipedia). The following season, he would make a life-changing move. He was hired by George Steinbrenner to manage the New York Yankees. Over twelve seasons in the Bronx, he would lead the Yankees to four World Championship titles. After the 2007 season Torre was offered --what many considered an insult --an incentive laden contract to stay in New York and turned it down. Instead he decided to join the Los Angeles Dodgers where he would finish his managerial career before joining the Commissioner's Office in New York.

Tony LaRussa is yet another Hall of Fame skipper who was hired and fired over the years. His first managerial job was in Chicago with the White Sox. He managed the Sox from 1979-1986 and was named the AL Manager of the Year in 1983 but he was fired in 1986 after his club got off to a slow start. That same season he would join the Oakland A's as their skipper. He managed the A's from 1986-1995 leading them to three straight World Series appearances from 1988-1990. In 1996 he would replace Joe Torre in St. Louis and lead the Cardinals to two World Series titles (2006 and 2011) (baseball reference). He would retire as manager of the Cardinals after winning his third World Championship in 2011. After working on the field he has now transitioned to the Arizona Diamondbacks front office with an advisory role.

Dusty Baker managed the San Francisco Giants from1993 to 2002. In 2002 he led the Giants to a World Series berth but failed to win the title and the Giants did not offer him a contract to return.

He joined the Cubs in 2003 and finished there in 2006. Despite leading the 2003 Cubs to their first division title in a decade he could not keep his team in the playoffs and he was not offered a contract to return in 2007. In 2010, Baker led the Reds to the playoffs for the first time in 15 seasons. He would finish his managerial career with the Cincinnati Reds in 2013 being fired after losing the wild card game to the Pirates that year. After a brief hiatus he returned to managing being named the skipper of the Washington Nationals in November of 2015. He led the Nationals to an NL East title but the team was eliminated from the 2016 playoffs after the first round.

What all of these men have in common is perseverance. The same perseverance that other managers such as Davey Johnson, Buck Showalter and Bruce Bochy shared. Football head coaches Bill Parcells and Tony Dungy also share the distinction of being hired and fired as head coaches. Some of the most successful people and companies in our country have had their ups and downs. If you look at scientists and inventors like Albert Einstein, Thomas Edison and Henry Ford, they all persevered. They all failed many times before finding success and discovering the theory of relativity, electricity and the single engine car. But, they did not give up. Just like Buck Showalter has not given up despite managing his fourth organization. He left the Yankees and Diamondbacks a year before they won the World Series. After managing the Rangers, he returned to the broadcast booth and was wooed back to the field by the Orioles. Now he is trying again to win, this time attempting to lead the O's to the post-season and a World Championship.

In the business world, some of the most successful companies have tried and tried again. Many thought the idea of a coffee company like Starbucks would never succeed. Starbucks first opened as a single store in Seattle's Pike Place Market back in 1971. Today there are more than 22,000 retail stores in more than 67 countries (Starbucks.com). The company's mission statement explains the success of Starbucks: "To inspire and nurture the human spirit-one person, one cup and one neighborhood at a time."

The values of the company also parallel a successful sports team. Take a look at how the Starbucks Company describes itself. "With our partners, our coffee and our customers at our core, we live these values: Creating a culture of warmth and belonging, where everyone is welcome. Acting with courage, challenging the status quo and finding new ways to grow our company and each other. Being present, connecting with transparency, dignity and respect. Delivering our very best in all we do, holding ourselves accountable for results. We are performance driven, through the lens of humanity."

All of these values are alive in sports as well. Launching a product is challenging. Businesses such as The FedEx Company and McDonalds have re-branded themselves over the years. Many businesses have had to start over when jumping back into the market. They fail, regroup and push forward. Sports teams and players have done the same.

On a personal level, what are some of the thoughts that run through most people's minds when they hear the words "you're fired", "we're going in a different direction", "we need a new voice" or the game simply decides for you by age that those once God-given profitable skill sets are no longer meeting the margin for success and you are "released" and the playing days are over. The music has stopped. Immediate thoughts are most likely, "What's next and am I prepared for what's next?"

The answers to these questions and many more sports and life related questions will be discussed in Real Excellence (RE) Sports Volume 1: *The End Game* by Bo Porter.

Sports is a career with a timeline, but education, character, leadership and professionalism will last a lifetime! *The End Game* goes beyond "play ball" and focuses on the lifelong attributes an athlete needs to succeed on and off the field and especially in future endeavors.

When you look at the overall success of people that have gone on to accomplish greatness in many walks of life, it is proven that some of their greatest experience and character development was gained by participating in competitive sports. Our country's greatest leaders have benefited from sports and competition. Gerald Ford played on two College National Championship football teams at Michigan in the 1930's and President George H.W. Bush played baseball at Yale and participated in the first two College World Series in the 1940's. John F Kennedy was a letter winning swimmer at Harvard and like many U.S. Presidents he shared a fondness for hitting the golf course. (Chase, 2013)

Competition is something leaders across the globe thrive on.

When you look at the professional world of sports today you can see how people are molded from coaches and teammates along the way. You can also see the impact sports have had on athletes from a business standpoint. From Michael Jordan and his Nike brand to Danica Patrick who has been able to parlay her sports career into the entertainment business, athletes are learning to communicate and get along with others and that helps them branch out into fields both inside and outside of their particular sport.

The End Game will look at Sports from four quadrants. When properly executed these four quadrants will provide whole person development and a bridge to your success in all aspects of your life. The four quadrants are "The REason" we play sports and why sports exist, "The REsponsibility" of all parties involved and how and why they are charged to impact the development of those playing sports, "The REality" of a career in sports and "The REwards" that one should strive to achieve when participating in sports. Bo Porter's book *The End Game* will analyze what REal Excellence looks like and the results of those that master "The End Game".

When you finish reading *The End Game* I hope you also gain a better understanding of how you, too, can give back and make a difference like Bo Porter has over the years.

TABLE OF CONTENTS

ACKNOWLEDGMENTS

God: First and foremost, I want to thank my Heavenly Father for sending His only son to be my Lord and Savior. In my life's journey, God has met me wherever I was spiritually and sent the right people into my life every step of the way. I am so thankful for Your mercy and grace. May Your will be done with the publishing of *The End Game*. To God be all the glory.

Bryce: Getting this book to home plate has been extremely costly in more ways than I even desire to admit. I'm not talking about monetary cost. The cost I'm referring to is more valuable than money. Actually it's priceless! When the 2016 MLB season came to an end October 2nd for the Atlanta Braves, my son Bryce Porter was anxiously awaiting my arrival at home. It was officially the off-season and that means father and son time, fun, football, school drop-off and pickup and lots of basketball. The MLB season is extremely challenging for families, especially when you live in Texas and work in Atlanta.

So this is more of a confession, apology and life lesson all wrapped up into a project that has reopened my eyes to the importance of work-life balance and time management - two components that resonated in my heart as I was rounding third and heading home with *The End Game*.

The first three weeks of my off-season was a complete whirlwind and at times I stopped and questioned if I could continue with this project. I thought I was putting myself through hell but in reality I was putting my family through it. I was irritable, preoccupied and unreasonable. I was late for one of Bryce's basketball games, I missed a deadline for an important event and wanted to blame everyone but myself.

I felt like a selfish jerk and for good reason, because I was one. At one point I even thought about canceling the scheduled book release. But quitting has never been a part of my DNA since that "Beverly Porter tongue lashing of 1977". More on that in Chapter One.

How did this happen? I had *The End Game* manuscript on second base with nobody out a year ago. Well, a lot can happen in a year. We grow, we encounter new relationships, we witness the outcomes of decisions

i

by others and ourselves. All this newfound content caused me to restructure some of the chapters and that lead to an enormous amount of unexpected work. But like the determined athlete, I rolled up my sleeves and accepted the challenge. So for three weeks I found myself against the clock to meet the new October 24th deadline of the publishing company. This is after the publishing company had already given me a two-week extension.

With perseverance and determination on my side I worked around-the-clock seven days a week trying to get my manuscript finished and at the same time manage my day-to-day responsibilities. I tried everything to maximize my productivity. I woke up at 5am every morning, locked myself in my office at home to get away from distractions. My breaks consisted of taking Bryce to school, a trip to Starbucks and I brought my work with me everywhere I went. I had to miss watching America's favorite team, the Dallas Cowboys, on Sundays. It was the off-season, time to relax, vacation, workout with and watch my son play basketball, and enjoy the family. We had been on the go since Spring Training started the second week of February. But here I was passing my son, like a ship in the night. On the way by he would ask, "Daddy, are you almost finished?" I would reply, "We're almost home free!"

Now that I've made it home and the manuscript is in the hands of the publishing company, I realize I'm behind on the one of the most important scoreboards – the father and son scoreboard and my daily scoreboard with God's word.

I can't in good conscience give you advice on work-life balance and time management when I didn't practice what I preach for a month into my off-season. I'm sharing this with my readers because it would be irresponsible not to share. It can also be an enlightening read and teaching tool for the next aspiring writer, entrepreneur and highly driven professional.

I'm home free, my son was loving and forgiving and our off-season is in full swing. What I do know is that by NOT having to write and instead being active, connecting, engaging and serving others I've gotten back into my daily routine of morning prayer sessions with God's word.

I now sit in my office and focus on the many responsibilities of my new position as Special Assistant to the General Manager, our family off-season schedule and growing my business conglomerate Real Excellence

Inc.

I'm now refreshed and focused. *The End Game* lesson: You can't redline your engine all the time and expect your performance not to suffer. We need to step back in order to stay productive and creative. More isn't more, less is more...it helps you have more focus and productivity when you resume your work.

I've already apologized to Bryce and he accepted my apology with open and loving arms. I'm blessed that he didn't charge my behavior to his heart. His forgiveness has allowed me to enjoy the fruits of labor getting *The End Game* to home plate safely.

I believe this book will be an amazing resource for so many and that God orchestrated this entire process. It is easy to become overwhelmed with big projects but never become so consumed that it takes away from the fabric of your responsibility to be an active, participating and engaging, valuable addition for your family and those who share space with you.

This is how your kids fill your heart and give you confirmation! This is a text message I received from my son, Bryce:

> *Thank you daddy for the message and I will do what you told me to do. I'm gonna have a great day and care for others and I hope you have a great day too! I hope you miss me and I love you and I hope you have a great great great week! And daddy you are the best and thank you for practicing basketball with me before you left to Atlanta. And thank you for everything you give me. Thank you for your help and I will have a great week and you mean a lot to me. You're the best dad I could ever have. Love Bryce* ❤

We are safe at home and there's no place like home. Enjoy *The End Game*!

Beverly Porter: My loving mother and the strongest woman I know. Witnessing you overcome the many obstacles and circumstances in your life truly helped shape and mold my mental toughness, work ethic and fortitude. Mother, you taught me so many valuable life lessons, but the one that resonates in my mind over and over again happened when I was seven years old. The details of this story will be discussed later in the book but the life lesson from this "Beverly Porter tongue lashing" was transformational. The roundup lashing came after you witnessed me sitting on the front porch, when I was supposed to be playing with the other kids. Mother, you said, "I'm not raising a quitter. If I was a quitter, you nor I would be here. The only thing quitting guarantees is that you will never know if you were good enough to accomplish what you set out to achieve. Remember this feeling of defeat and allow it to motivate you in your preparation. Before you ever think about quitting, ask yourself why you started in the first place". And last but surely not the least of your transformational words you said to me were, "I'm your mother and I love you unconditionally but your teammates and the kids you're playing with will not be as forgiving because no one likes a quitter." Mother, thank you for your honesty and unconditional love.

Holly Chervnsik: Founder and Owner of SuburbanBuzz Publishing - Holly, your experience, knowledge and collaboration helped me turn a life spent in sports into a powerful masterpiece. Thank you for your time, effort and patience throughout this entire project. Your finishing touches added visual images that will resonate in the minds of our readers. I'm thankful and forever grateful for all you put into getting this project safely to home plate. Great job and congratulations!

Shaye Henderson: Chief Editor and Data Researcher - Shaye, thank you for your tireless efforts, data research and editorial expertise. Your attention to detail and literary guidance throughout this project kept me on track. Your commitment to excellence can be found in the completion of *The End Game*. I was truly blessed to have you as the chief editor for *REal Life EMPOWERED* and now *The End Game*. This book reveals and discusses plenty of my personal stories but your personal touch helped bring the stories to life for our readers. I'm already looking forward to our next project. I'm thankful and forever grateful for all you put into making this project come to life. The next Starbucks is on me! Great job and congratulations!

Debbi Taylor: Co-Writer and Exclusive Interviewer - Debbi, it seems like yesterday we were discussing the possibility of writing *The End Game* in the dugout at Nationals Park in Washington, DC. Your encouragement, insight and guidance helped formulate the transformational messages delivered in *The End Game*. I thank you for all your time and effort with gathering the content that brought this book to life. Your commitment to travel around the country and conduct interviews was admirable. Your professional interviews provided confirmation and quotes throughout the book that helped legitimize the content in *The End Game*. I'm thankful and forever grateful to have someone of your experience and expertise co-author this book. We have delivered a powerful resource for our readers. Great job and congratulations!

Minister Irving Johnson: My earthly father and whose life story is the best living example known to me of God meeting one of His children where they are and bringing them home. My dad's spiritual journey has been an inspiration for me to live my life for Christ. My dad always ends our conversations by saying these three things: "Keep Christ first in your life and you will always have a life", "Kiss your wife and hug your son" and "Daddy loves you!"

Baseball Chapel: My church away from home. Being blessed with an opportunity to have a career in sports means I travel a great portion of the year. With travel comes a lot of Sundays and Wednesdays without attending my traditional church service. Baseball Chapel has been the Spiritual food for many professional baseball players over the years. I want to thank all of our Chapel leaders, but I want to especially thank Tim Pierson, our Chapel leader in Washington DC, when I coached for the Washington Nationals. Tim's commitment to sharing God's Word and the personal interest he took in connecting and engaging in my Spiritual development was transformative.

David Yasko: My Minister at Westbury Church of Christ and one of my most faithful prayer warriors - David, your support, wisdom and prayers have always been uplifting. You are more than my Minister, you are my brother and a dear friend.

Bill Yasko: My retired Minister from Westbury Church of Christ, and the man who bore witness to two of the greatest days of my earthly life. Bill was the minister responsible for bringing me to Christ in baptism and the minister whom we choose to officiate our wedding. Thank you for loving me as Christ loves the church.

Michael Porter: If the people of Newark, NJ and the surrounding area were polled and asked, "Was Michael Porter an NBA talent?" I believe the result would be a resounding "Yes"! My Uncle Michael in my opinion is one of the best players to have never played in the NBA. His possible NBA career was cut short by an unfortunate knee injury, but not before he had a chance to help his nephew fall in love with basketball. I was five years old but I vividly remember going from gym to gym and playground to playground watching my Uncle Michael play. In between games my uncle would let me shoot until the next game started. My love for sports was developed and nurtured at a very young age. Uncle Michael, thank you for dragging me from gym to gym and playground to playground. I also want you to know your personal story has always been a positive motivating factor in my life. Having witnessed first-hand how an injury can end the career of a potential professional athlete truly helped me understand the priceless value of education.

Interviewees: We would like to thank the following people for their dedication to sports and education and for giving us their much appreciated time, insights and thoughtful responses to all of our interview requests:

Bob Carpenter, Television Voice of the Washington Nationals Baseball Club

Donna E. Cohen, Esquire. Founder and Principal, Donna Cohen Strategies

Bob Elliott, Assistant to the head coach, University of Notre Dame and Bo's Defensive Back Coach at Iowa

Robert Fondren, SELF Foundation Board of Directors, Texas Hawkeyes Alum, Completions Engineer

Frank Gavin, Retired teacher and Bo's High School Basketball coach

Kenneth Hughes, Greenpark Compounding Pharmacy & Gifts

Nancy Hughes, SELF Foundation Board of Directors, Greenpark Compounding Pharmacy & Gifts

Cliff King, Teammate University of Iowa football team, Regional Field Manager for Nike Sports Marketing

Jessica Kissane, (Ph.D. Psychologist) Stay at Home Mom, part time Adjunct Psychology Professor at Stetson University

Trey Forkerway, Regional Scout for the Chicago Cubs and Bo's ex-teammate

Cameron Maybin, MLB Outfielder, Los Angeles Angels

Carlos Pena, Retired MLB player, current MLB Network Analyst

Beverly Porter, Bo Porter's mom

Bobby Scales, Special Assistant to the General Manager for the Los Angeles Angels

Boz Walker, Longtime Newark, NJ resident and friend of "Mr. Miller" Bo's first little league coach

Linda Wawrzyniak, President of Higher Standards Academy

Dave Winfield, Hall of Fame Baseball Player, Business Advisor, Management Consultant, Author and Keynote Speaker

INTRODUCTION

Growing up on Avon Avenue and South 14th Street in Newark, NJ (aka Brick City) was unpredictable, yet predictable. You could predict that you would hear gun shots, police sirens, loud music and that drugs were being sold on most every corner.

The unpredictable storylines are what made growing up in Newark unimaginable to many and unsurvivable for me without God's calling in my life. How are these storylines for unpredictable: Without notice a car chase could break out at any moment; car theft was a popular crime in Newark and the police chase at times ended with innocent bystanders or drivers being killed. On a hot summer night one such chase ended the life of one of my closest childhood friends - he was 18 years old. When I was 13 years old, I was lying in bed watching television and heard four gun shots outside my open window. I did the normal drill and jumped on the floor in fear. Moments later with police sirens blaring and ambulances surrounding the parking lot I found out my seventeen-year-old childhood friend had been robbed, shot and killed. As the police covered his body and tears poured down the faces of family and friends, I sat on my front porch scared, heartbroken and confused. At the age of 14, as a friend of mine and I were walking to the corner store we were robbed at gunpoint. These random crimes of unpredictability can lead one to hope, wish and wonder how in the world can one ever get out of these circumstances.

There is a saying, "Ships don't sink because of the water around them, ships sink because of the water that gets in them." Although I was growing up in an environment where crime, mischief and unfortunate mishaps seemed like the norm, I never allowed the water to get in my ship. I was hopeful that my storyline would not be another Newark "unpredictable but predictable" outcome. For years I not only wondered how I survived the streets of Newark but also I often found myself asking why did He choose me.

In my book *The End Game*, I will reveal how God and sports lifted me up from an environment of unpredictable circumstances and delivered me to a platform from which I could glorify His Kingdom. *The End Game* draws from my life experience which includes twenty-three plus years in professional sports as a player, coach, manager, television network analyst, mentor, business owner and philanthropist. My book analyzes what REAL EXCELLENCE in sports and life looks like and why some players have managed to master "The End Game".

God doesn't give us all the same circumstances, the same job, the same kind of family, the same environment in which to live. Since we are all unique individuals, He treats us differently in order to bring each of us to Him. But He loves us all the same and desires the same salvation for us all. The Bible says, "You are all children of God through faith in Christ Jesus. And all who have been united with Christ in baptism have put on Christ, like putting on new clothes...You are all one in Christ Jesus." GALATIANS 3:26-28

My storyline began in Newark, but it will live forever because the lessons I learned in and through sports have given me a servant heart, an inspired determination to positively impact the lives of others, and the humility to know that I didn't do it; He did! Having God-given ability to play sports is one thing but understanding that sports is an institution of higher learning is transformational. I pray *The End Game* resonates in your heart, inspires your soul and empowers you to use the valuable lessons learned in sports to edify others.

The REason – DEVELOPMENTAL LEVEL

Testimony

Laurie Nicolai - August 17, 2015:

My son participated in Bo Porter's baseball program from the age of 14 to 18. Undeniably a very important and formative time in his life.

Without a doubt his baseball program was unlike any we had seen or heard of before. Just by watching the practices alone you could see they were on a very different level of dedication and attention to detail. Trey not only learned the mechanics of baseball but the underlying strategy of the coach's decisions. His knowledge of baseball is far superior than most due to the teachings of Bo and his staff.

However, there were far more important benefits he acquired which he can use for a lifetime off the field. The words that come to mind are commitment, critical thinking skills, time management, and a desire to challenge himself to reach his goals. He spent time around Bo who demonstrated a healthy lifestyle and a strong commitment to faith and family.

Besides their children's attitudes focusing on their future they can expect to hear often.....''Well, Bo says this (fill in the blank) and Bo says that (fill in the blank) which will be a repeating of uplifting, goal oriented quotes and which by the way he can still repeat 10 years later. I am forever thankful that Bo and his program were part of Trey's upbringing and believe he is a better man for it.

I strongly suggest and recommend Bo Porter and his program to any parent.

CHAPTER 1: INTRODUCTION TO SPORTS IN SOCIETY | DEVELOPMENT PRACTICES

The life lessons learned in sports are plentiful but one has to be willing to learn as the educational process unfolds. What is education? Is it different from schooling? When researching the definition of education, I found a number of different definitions. The definition of education by Merriam-Webster dictionary is: *the action or process of teaching someone especially in a school, college, or university; the knowledge, skill, and understanding that you get from attending a school, college, or university.* Oxford dictionary defines education as: *a body of knowledge acquired while being educated.* Dictionary.com defines education as: *the act or process of imparting or acquiring general knowledge, developing the powers of reasoning and judgment, and generally of preparing oneself or others intellectually for mature life.*

For many people the importance of education lies in future job prospects, for others it is quality of citizenship, and yet others just want literacy, critical thinking, and/or creativity. I believe that behind the many different definitions of education is one fundamental idea: an educated person is someone who perceives accurately, thinks clearly, and acts effectively on selected goals. When talking about education people often confuse it with schooling. Many think of places like schools or colleges when seeing or hearing the word. The most known educational curriculum system consists of classes such as: math, reading, English, science, social studies, history.

It is often said that we are learning all the time and that we may not be conscious of it happening. Learning is both a process and an outcome. As a process you are taking the steps to gathering information. It is part of living in the world, part of the way our minds and bodies work. As an outcome it is a new understanding or appreciation of something, which leads to the fundamental concept I want to convey about education as it relates to sports. The education you are privileged to gain from participating in sports will come from a special institution of higher learning. Your desire to apply and use this transformational knowledge will determine the grade you receive from the Master on your final exam at the gates of Heaven. You are now signed up for and enrolled in an institution that has produced more impactful people than any college or university. You are officially on stage. Let the GAME begin!

Whenever you think about the foundation of success, the word *fundamental* is often associated with the development level. In sports mastering the fundamentals is paramount to your overall success. When it comes to competition, I've always believed that the most fundamentally sound person or team has the best chance to achieve success. The development level of sports is filled with teachable moments that later become the core fabric of one of your most important traits, "your character." You will be called upon to practice these fundamental characteristics daily. I'm sure you have heard the phase, "Practice makes perfect". What I believe is "Practice doesn't make perfect but perfect practice will make permanent." Practice is where you learn and develop.

One of my most memorable, teachable moments in sports happened when I was seven years old. The coach/teacher was my mother, Beverly Porter. It was a hot summer day and several friends and I were playing our usual pick-up game of baseball in the church parking lot on 14th Street. It was the last inning, two outs, bases were loaded and I was at bat. I was always the youngest of the boys who played in the parking lot. The games in the church parking lot were never short on talent, intensity or a controversial call that usually caused an argument.

This was 1979, so unlike today when a call is objected, a team can invoke a replay challenge and get the call right. There was no replay, we didn't even have official umpires for our pick-up games in the church parking lot. We made the out or safe, ball or strike, and fair or foul calls ourselves. Having no umpires was the beginning of this story but the lesson learned was far more valuable that day than instant replay could have ever been. So here's what happened:

I hit what appeared to me and those on my team to be a game winning grand slam home run down the left field line over the light pole across the street. However, the opposing team called the hit a foul. Let me state one major factor about the light pole we considered the foul pole: unlike on a regulated baseball field, it wasn't straight down the third base line. With that said, I was seven and the joy of getting the game winning hit was rushing through my body.

After arguing back and forth for a good five minutes, the two team captains decided to do what we always did when a controversial call could not be decided. The unwritten rule to settle any call was to flip a coin. So the two older players came together at home plate to flip the coin. Well, we lost the coin flip, which meant my so-called game winning home run didn't count and I had to get back in the box and continue my at bat. What happened next changed the course of my life forever!

I was so upset and mad about the outcome of the coin flip I grabbed my bat and my glove and left. Simply stated, I quit because the call didn't go my way. I walked home with tears pouring down my face and ignored the calling of my friends, "Bo come back, Bo come back." When I arrived at my house, my mother was inside the kitchen cooking and heard me crying on the front porch. She came out and asked, "What are you crying about?" After explaining the story, my seven-year-old mind was expecting some moral support from my mom. Wrong! The coach/teacher/parent came out full blast and Beverly Porter unloaded a tongue lashing on me for the ages. "I'm not raising a quitter. If I was a quitter, you nor I would be here. The only thing quitting guarantees is that you will never know if you were good enough to accomplish what you set out to achieve. Remember this feeling of defeat and allow it to motivate you in your preparation. Before you ever think about quitting, ask yourself why you started in the first place. Quitting is poor sportsmanship". And last but surely not the least of her transformational words she said to me were, "I'm your mother and I love you unconditionally but your teammates and the kids you're playing with will not be as forgiving because no one likes a quitter. Now get back down there, apologize and finish your game. The outcome doesn't matter. You can live and learn from any outcome, but I will not allow you to be a quitter."

So I walked back down to the church parking lot and apologized to all the boys. They accepted my apology and we agreed to continue the game. After the foul ball, it was now two strikes, two outs, bases loaded and I was down to my last strike. I ended up striking out to end the game and we lost!

That night after dinner my mom came into my room and asked about the continuation and outcome of the game. I told her what happened and she asked a question that my seven-year-old brain would have never thought to include in my evaluation of why I struck out. She asked, "Were you still mad about the call when you struck out?" "Yes", I said. She then said, "It's hard to perform and focus when your mind is someplace else. The next time you find yourself in a situation like that, you have to let that go and focus on what you're trying to accomplish." I was in the second grade and my educational classes at the time centered around math, weekly spelling tests and reading comprehension. But I must admit, this entire situation taught me some valuable life lessons that I wasn't receiving in school:

1. I learned the importance of good sportsmanship.
2. I learned to apologize when I'm wrong.
3. I learned that quitting was not an acceptable action.
4. I learned that you have to move past disappointment and anger if you want to have a chance to accomplish the next task.
5. I learned that I could use a negative outcome as an opportunity to grow.
6. I witnessed my mother's unconditional love!

I'm thankful my mother used this sporting event to teach me these valuable life lessons. My experiences in sports have played a major role in my overall development. Throughout this book I will continue to share personal stories, interview quotes and research to bring even more credibility to all the good sports have to offer. Here are a few more fundamental character traits you should look to learn in your developmental level of sports:

- **Take Care of Number One:** The person you will spend the most time with in your life is yourself, so you better take care of *Number One*. It is impossible to help someone else if you can't help yourself. "At the end of the day, you're responsible for yourself and your actions and that's all you can control. So rather than be frustrated with what you can't control, try to fix the things you can." --Kevin Garnett
- **Desire:** "The starting point of all achievement is desire. Keep this constantly in mind. Weak desire brings weak results, just as a small amount of fire makes a small amount of heat." --Napoleon Hill
- **Practice:** "The will to success is important, but what's more important is the will to prepare." --Bobby Knight
- **Listen:** "The best players are the best listeners. Listen up, be coachable and teachable." --Mike Krzyzewski
- **Be Driven:** "Excellence is a gradual result of always striving to do

better." --Pat Riley
- **Perseverance:** "There's winning and there's losing and in life both will happen. What is never acceptable to me is quitting." --Earvin "Magic" Johnson
- **Teamwork:** "It's not about any one person. You've got to get over yourself and realize that it takes a group to get this thing done." --Greg Popovich
- **Time Management:** "People often complain about lack of time when the lack of direction is the real problem." --Zig Ziglar
- **Commitment:** "There's a difference between interest and commitment. When you're interested in doing something, you do it only when it's convenient. When you're committed to something you accept no excuses; only results." --Kenneth Blanchard
- **Critical Thinking:** "The number one thing we look for is general cognitive ability, and it's not IQ. It's learning ability. It's the ability to process on the fly." --Lazlo Bock

These character traits and more can and will be learned at some point throughout your journey in sports. As you navigate through life you will find the lessons learned become irreplaceable, invaluable, and life altering.

Here is what Carlos Pena, a retired MLB player and current MLB Network Analyst, had to say when asked, "How did sports help prepare you for life?"

"Sports prepare you for life. Sports prepare you for real life. What I mean by that is the real stuff being a father, being a husband, being a good contributor to society, dealing with life. For example, through sports you have perseverance. Perseverance is one of those things if you go through trials in life it gives you a platform or opportunity to put into practice: courage, how to deal with pain, failure and it gives you the luxury that you're dealing with it in an arena that it's not life or death. Your whole life is not hanging on it."

CHAPTER 2: CRITICAL FACTORS OF SUCCESS | PSYCHOLOGY OF VISUALIZATION

When the University of Iowa hired Hayden Fry in 1979, they had experienced 17 straight non-winning seasons. Fry turned his attention to changing a losing attitude and started new traditions at Iowa. He hired a marketing group to create the Tigerhawk, a logo to represent the University of Iowa athletic programs. He asked the Pittsburg Steelers for permission to use the black and gold colors to overhaul the uniforms in Steelers colors because at the time the Steelers were a dominant NFL team. He had the players swarm onto the field and even painted the visitor's locker room pink. Fry, a psychology major at Baylor, knew that pink is occasionally used to relax and pacify the residents in mental institutions. When all was said and done, Hayden Fry compiled a career college football record of 232-178-10. He is one of the greatest coaches in college football history and was enshrined into the College Football Hall of Fame in 2003. His accomplishments are astonishing: his coaching tree is one of the most distinguished among former head coaches, he had one of the highest graduation rates of any college football coach during his career and countless people still talk about Hayden's tenure at Iowa as one of the greatest turnarounds in college football history.

The Fry Psychological Impact

The Hawk Trot / The Swarm: "I wanted the players to feel like they were part of a family, to be conscious of that controlled togetherness as they made that slow entrance onto the field. It had a great psychological effect on the opposing team, too. They'd never seen anything like it." -- Hayden Fry

The Pink Locker Room: "It's been fun to get the reaction of visiting coaches to the color of the locker room. Most don't notice it, but those that do are in trouble.... When I talk to an opposing coach before a game and he mentions the pink walls, I know I've got him. I can't recall a coach who has stirred up a fuss about the color and then beat us." -- Hayden Fry

My decision to attend the University of Iowa and play football and baseball was one of the most important decisions in my life. The critical building blocks needed for success were instilled, nurtured, and carefully designed to prepare all the student-athletes to become champions in life. Coach Hayden Fry used the power of visualization and winning the psychological game better than anyone I've ever known. The "Hawk Trot" and the pink walls in the visitor's locker room are a few examples of how Hayden was able to create a sense of togetherness for our team and a distraction for the opposing teams.

But one of the most transformational lessons I learned at Iowa is something I believe everyone should practice daily. It was my first game at the University of Iowa and I must admit, I had a million thoughts running through my mind. As I sat at my locker receiving the final instructions from Coach Bob Elliott, my position coach, Coach Fry walked to the center of the locker room and said, "Everyone take a knee, bow your head, lock hands with your neighbor and repeat after me." He led us in the Lord's Prayer, which was comforting in itself, but after we finished the Lord's Prayer, Coach Fry said to turn out the lights and instructed everyone to close their eyes. "Now imagine yourself making big plays, intercepting a pass, scoring a touchdown and imagine the Hawkeyes winning and celebrating after the game. Turn the lights on, open your eyes and let's go win a football game." I had played sports my entire life but never did I feel more prepared and confident jogging onto the field at Kinnick Stadium than that beautiful day in September.

Hayden Fry had just opened my eyes to a newfound world. Visualization increases our chances of success-not just in sports but in any area of life. In a book written by Stephen Richards, *Think Your Way to Success: Let Your Dreams Run Free*, he wrote, "Once we open our eyes to the infinite magic that the universe has in abundance, we are sure to be enthralled by what we see and this miraculous creation gets us closer to our dreams and to the world as a whole."

The Power of Self-Realization

"What I always feared has happened to me. What I dreaded has come true." JOB 3:25

You have the ability to paint a picture of what life is going to look like. You may not get all the details exactly right, but you certainly have a part in shaping your future. Your prospective today has a lot to do with what happens tomorrow. What you believe and what you expect have a tendency to happen. That is why you should NEVER picture yourself failing, because if you do, you will have to experience the failure TWICE. The landscape of our future is in large part determined by what we think it will be and how you see yourself in it. This is "the power of self-realization", which study after study seems to validate. That doesn't mean you can manipulate your future, but there is a strong connection between your perceptions and your outcomes. Those who have positive expectations experience positive results more often than those who have negative expectations. Envision your future, your accomplishments and achievements, and your God-given significance. Base it on what you know to be true, of course, not on your own sense of pride or unhealthy ways to satisfy your needs, but within the values and dreams God has given you. With God's help - His power, encouragement, and energy flowing through our lives along with the gifts, abilities, and talents He has given us - we can shape the future. Because He created us, we have the potential of living lives of significance, possibility and impact. For better or worse, what you envision often begins to take shape.

Thinking

If you *think* you are beaten, you are,
If you *think* you dare not, you don't;
If you like to win, but *think* you can't,
It is almost a cinch you won't.

If you *think* you'll lose, you're lost,
For out in the world we find,
Success begins with a fellow's will-
It's all in his *state of mind*.

If you *think* you are outclassed, you are,
You've got to *think* high to rise;
You've got to be *sure of yourself* before
You can ever win a prize.

Life's battles don't always go
To the stronger or faster man,
But soon or late, the man who wins
Is the one who *thinks* he can!

--Walter D. Wintle

Studies show that the development of personality tends to be set by the time children are in the first grade or around six years old. The influence of their parents, home environment and events that happen to them will shape the bulk of their personality for the rest of their lives. Personality can be changed but once set, it becomes a very difficult feat to accomplish. The reason it is so important to understand this research is because too often parents, adults, coaches and teachers prevent children from growing and learning by not challenging our children to push themselves to grow and learn in exciting ways. Children's minds should be challenged so that they gain the ability to think and create ways to be successful or experiences that force them to ask questions and find their own way. When children are constantly handed success, grades, gifts, trophies, ribbons or "success" with no effort on their part we are actually stifling their growth and it can actually hinder their potential for success for the rest of their lives. Children must be taught the skills needed to foster success in their future.

One of the most important skills that children can learn is the ability to visualize what they want in their lives. The art of visualization is a natural concept to a child and we see it through their imagination as they play games as small children but as time goes on many of them lose this skill as their lives become more complex and more about "what they see" rather than what they can imagine. The conscious mind believes whatever we tell it and the subconscious holds onto all the experiences of our lives and becomes the "dictator" of the conscious mind. It tells the conscious mind what to think and how to react to the world around us based on our past experiences.

Although this is a wonderful set up and it can make our lives much easier to navigate because we're not constantly "reinventing the wheel" it can also be a negative thing because we can cease to grow and change if all of our current responses are based on past experiences. This is where the ability to visualize the things and experiences that you want are so very important when wanting them to come to fruition. Visualizing ourselves as successful or healthy sends thoughts to our conscious minds that whatever we are visualizing has already taken place. When the conscious mind begins to believe that these events are possible or have already happened the conscious mind will then send out signals to the mind and body to make them come to pass.

This is a type of confidence that is needed to create and sustain mental toughness or mental focus. Teaching children not to get caught up in what they can see but to have faith in the unseen and that whatever they believe is already done and on its way. Visualization works out to be a type of "faith" in one's abilities to manifest their own beliefs and desires. If a child can master this at a young age, then this skill will only grow and become stronger in time and success in their life and their dreams will surely manifest. But for these skills to flourish we as adults need to guide children but also allow them to navigate through their own challenges and learn to visualize and work towards creating their own answers with only guidance and encouragement on the part of the parents, teachers and coaches. Allowing children to grow in this manner is sure to foster successful confident adults with a healthy sense of intrinsic worth and confidence gained only by trial and error.

That's Why I'm Here!

In the Spring of 1995, I was faced with some major decisions. MLB was in the middle of a labor lockout that saw the 1994 season cut short. Spring Training in 1995 opened without the Major League roster players. Organizations were trying to fill the ML rosters with the best available talent. With opening day looming, organizations were set to open the 1995 MLB season with "Replacement Players". The question came down from Major League Camp asking who would be willing to cross the line and play if the strike continued into the season? Those who agreed to be Replacement Players would be paid additional funds by the organization. Because this was my first Spring Training, and I lacked extensive knowledge about the strike and the CBA (Collective Bargaining Agreement) I starting asking plenty of questions, and those questions lead to a conversation that always brings me back to the power of education, self-realization and confidence. The most important information I gained by asking questions was what happens to players who cross the line. Well, here is the long and short of it: any player that crossed the line will never be allowed to be a member of the Player's Association. That is a major decision because the MLB Player's Association is directly attached to the MLB Pension. Asking questions is a major life lesson and one I will always share. If you don't know something, ask questions.

My locker mate that spring was a fellow outfielder, who was a 3rd round draft pick in 1993 from Vanderbilt and a top prospect in the Cubs organization at the time. I was a 40th round draft pick in that same 1993 draft. My teammate asked me, "Hey are you going to take the money and cross the line if the strike continues into the season?" But because I asked questions and now had a better understanding of the consequences to crossing the line, I answered with a resounding, "No!" He then asked, "Why not?" I replied, "Because I want to be a part of the union when I get to the Big Leagues." The next few lines of this conversation would eventually define the professional baseball careers of this particular teammate and Bo Porter. My teammate then asked, "You believe you're going to play in the Big Leagues?" I replied, "That's why I'm here, and if I didn't believe I was going to play in the Big Leagues, I wouldn't be here." He never did give me a clear answer about why he would cross the line, but I remember leaving the conversation and saying to myself, "He doesn't believe he's going to play in the Big Leagues."

Well, fast forward 21 years and the proof of self-realization proves valuable once again. My teammate's professional career ended in 1997 at the Double-A level and I played in the Major Leagues with the Chicago Cubs, Oakland A's and the Texas Rangers. After retiring as a player in 2003, I begin my coaching career in 2005 and on April 23rd of the 2016 season I reached 10 years of Major League pension service time. The significance of this blessing from a monetary perspective is great for my family and me. But I can't help but think back to that conversation during Spring Training 1995 and how paramount that decision would be in my life. As I sit here today, I can honestly say this teammate had more talent than I did, but this further provides concrete evidence of the power of one's mind. There was never a day I didn't believe that I would play in the Big Leagues.

Felix Unger and Oscar Madison Move Over – There is a New Odd Couple in Town!

Ken Griffey Jr. and Mike Piazza were inducted into the Baseball Hall of Fame Class of 2016. The two took almost polar opposite paths to reach the Major Leagues. Griffey, the son of an All-Star, was drafted No.1 overall, and Piazza, the son of an Italian businessman, wasn't drafted until the 62nd round, the lowest to ever be inducted into the Hall of Fame.

So how do these two polar opposites reach the same pole at the same time? "We've taken the same path," Griffey said. "We got drafted, we worked hard in the Minor League system and we had an opportunity to become big-league ballplayers and produce. I grew up where my dad said, 'If you work hard and do things right, you're going to get rewarded.' "He said the hardest thing about playing Minor League ball is getting drafted, because not a lot of people get drafted. But once you get your foot in the door, anything goes. You're only a first-round pick for one year. There are more second-, third-, fourth-, fifth- and so on in the Big Leagues than first-round picks. So for me, you work day in and day out, don't take no for an answer, and be the best player you can be."

Apparently Mike Piazza was given the same speech and adopted the same work ethic. Piazza was 62nd round pick, with 1,389 players taken ahead of him in that 1988 June draft. "He had unique challenges, being a first-round pick," Piazza said of Griffey. "I had a unique challenge, being a last-round pick. There was pressure on him; there was pressure on me. Maybe a little different, or maybe nuanced a different way. ... For me, there was a challenge to my professional life. I knew I had to play well, because I knew I wasn't going to have a lot of leeway to fail, but it made me better."

During the induction ceremony Piazza spoke briefly to his dad in Italian, telling him, "Many thanks to the country of Italy for the gift of my father." "My father's faith in me, often greater than my own, is the single most important factor of me being inducted into this Hall of Fame."

Mike Piazza's father, Vince, so believed in his son's future he built a batting cage for him, and even had him go to sleep using hand grips to strengthen his hands. Vince was overcome with emotion when his son said, "We made it, Dad! The race is over. Now is the time to smell the roses."

Griffey is the first number one pick in a draft to reach Cooperstown. He played with his father in Seattle, and even played for his hometown team in Cincinnati where his dad was an integral part of "The Big Red Machine" of the 70s. Barely able to say the emotional words, Ken Griffey Jr. said during his acceptance speech, "My dad taught me how to play the game, but more importantly, he taught me to be a man."

So in the end these two men took very different paths to reach Cooperstown. But one thing they did have in common was a parent who encouraged them, loved them dearly, and instilled in them the payoff that surely can come from perseverance, hard work, visualization and dedication to a goal.

"When you talk about perseverance you talk about courage, you can talk about dealing with failure, you can talk about being resilient and getting up after failing and dusting yourself off. All those things are developed and maintained through sports because you're challenged in many ways." -- Carlos Pena

To sum it up:

Instincts - a player with great aptitude, feeling, gift, gut reaction, impulse, intuition, know-how, sixth sense, talent and tendency when it comes to accomplishing success in a particular area. Instincts are God-given and can happen in the blink of an eye.

Emotions - a player's mental attitude, disposition, feelings, inner nature, makeup, mentality, mindset, mood, spirits, state of mind, temper, temperament, and temporary psychological state. Your emotional state is usually a reactionary state of being, meaning something happens, a feeling comes over you and your next decision will determine your immediate state of being. Acknowledge your emotions but don't let them control your every action.

Psyche - directly related to one's self-esteem. If a player is not mentally strong their chance of reaching their full potential will be challenging and in most cases will not happen.

The Impact:

Uncontrolled emotions can have an adverse effect for competitive people who fail to master the psychological warfare that can take place in one's mind. It prohibits them from understanding the difference between instincts and emotions. Having good instincts can help a player achieve success but to reach your full potential those instincts must be accompanied by a strong mental psyche, fortitude and the ability to harness your emotions. To better understand the impact of harnessing your emotions and the power of winning the mental game visit Career in Sports Development Academy (CiSDA) website at www.careerinsportsda.com. Our RE-SPORTS Certified Instructor will provide the bridge you need to reach your full potential.

CHAPTER 3: INTERPERSONAL RELATIONSHIPS | SOCIETY AND SYNERGISTIC CULTURE

As it relates to team, one of the greatest sayings is, "Teamwork makes the dream work." --Unknown

In the business world teamwork is such a vital way of completing projects that it is worth developing and refining the skills that will help you make a valuable contribution to whatever type of team you are on. Sports teams are perfect examples of how many players working together can achieve much more than one player who is acting alone. Being a valuable team member can open new career opportunities because leaders may see firsthand what a great job you're doing. You may even be asked to bring your strengths into play in a higher profile business critical project. This is why learning to be a good team player is so important. Change, adaptability and getting along with others are key components of being a good teammate. If you make a good impression you never know what possibilities might open for you.

I have been a member of countless teams and I have always aimed to add value to any team. Throughout my career I've been blessed to witness both ends of the spectrum, as it relates to good and bad teammates. Interpersonal relationships and the ability to get along with people will determine the culture of any team.

Six Ways Successful Teams Are Built To Last

It takes great leadership to build great teams. Leaders who are not afraid to course correct, make the difficult decisions and establish standards of performance that are constantly being met – and improving at all times. Whether in the workplace, professional sports, or your local community, team building requires a keen understanding of people, their strengths and what gets them excited to work with others. Team building requires the management of egos and their constant demands for attention and recognition – not always warranted. Team building is both an art and a science and the leader who can consistently build high performance teams is worth their weight in gold.

History has shown us that it takes a special kind of leader with unique competencies and skills to successfully build great companies and teams. In the sports world, the late John Wooden set the standard for great coaches, leading UCLA to ten NCAA national basketball championships in a 12-year period — seven of which were in a row. His success was so iconic, Wooden created his own "Pyramid for Success" to help others excel through his proven wisdom. In the business world, we can look to Jack Welch, who was the Chairman and CEO of General Electric between 1981 and 2001. According to Wikipedia, the company's value rose 4000% during his tenure. In 2006 Welch's net worth was estimated at $720 million and in 2009 he launched the Jack Welch Management Institute at Strayer University.

Building companies requires the know-how to build long-lasting teams. This is why most managers never become leaders and why most leaders never reach the highest pinnacle of leadership success. It requires the ability to master the "art of people" and knowing how to maneuver hundreds (if not thousands) of people at the right place and at the right time. It means knowing how each person thinks and how to best utilize their competencies correctly at all times. It is playing a continuous chess match – knowing that every wrong move that is made can cost the company hundreds of thousands, if not millions of dollars (just ask BP and Enron).

As you evaluate the sustainability of the team(s) you lead and its real impact on the organization you serve, here are six ways successful teams are built to last:

1. **Be Aware of How You Work** - As the leader of the team, you must be extremely aware of your leadership style and techniques. Are they as effective as you think? How well are they accepted by the team you are attempting to lead? Evaluate yourself and be critical about where you can improve, especially in areas that will benefit those whom you are a leading.

   Though you may be in charge, how you work may not be appreciated by those who work with you. You may have good intentions, but make sure you hold yourself accountable to course-correct and modify your approach if necessary to assure that you are leading from a position of strength and respectability.

   Be your own boss. Be flexible. Know who you are as a leader.

2. **Get to Know the Rest of the Team** - Much like you need to hold yourself accountable for your actions to assure you maximize performance and results, you must make the time to get to know your team and encourage camaraderie. We must be caring, nurturing, understanding and embrace the needs of our team. Our number one goal in every relationship should be to help our teammates experience their significance.

   To do so we must gather intelligence. Gathering intelligence means learning what defines the strengths and capabilities of our team – the real assets that each member brings to the table, the traits they need to leave behind and those yet to be developed. Simply stated: get to know the people you are charged to lead.

   All great leaders know exactly what buttons to push and when to push them. They are experts at activating the talent that surrounds them. They are equally as effective at matching unique areas of subject matter expertise and/or competencies to solve problems and seek new solutions.

   Fully knowing your team means that you have invested the time to understand how they are wired to think and what is required to motivate them to excel beyond what is expected from them.

   Think of your team as puzzle pieces that can be placed together in a variety of ways.

3. **Clearly Define Roles and Responsibilities** - When you successfully complete Step 2, you can then more effectively and clearly define the roles and responsibilities of those on your team. Now, don't assume this is an easy step; in fact, you'll often find that people's ideal roles lie outside their job descriptions.

   Each of your team member's responsibilities must be interconnected and dependent upon one another. This is not unlike team sports, where some players are known as "system players" – meaning that, although they may not be the most talented person on the team, they know how to work best within the "system." This is why you must have a keen eye for talent that can evaluate people not only on their ability to play a particular role – but even more so on whether they fit the workplace culture (the system) and will be a team player. For example, I once inherited an employee who wasn't very good at his specific job. Instead of firing him, I took the time to get to know him and utilized his natural talents as a strategic facilitator who could keep all of the moving parts within the department in proper alignment and in lock-step communication. This person helped our team operate more efficiently and saved the company money by avoiding the bad decisions they previously made because of miscommunications. He was eventually promoted into a special projects manager role.

A team should operate as a mosaic whose unique strengths and differences convert into a powerful united force.

4. **Be Proactive with Feedback** - Feedback is the key to assuring any team is staying on track, but more importantly that it is improving each day. Feedback should be proactive and constant. Many leaders are prone to wait until a problem occurs before they give feedback.

Feedback is simply the art of great communication. It should be something that is part of one's natural dialogue. Feedback can be both formal and informal. In fact, if it becomes too structured and stiff, it becomes difficult for the feedback to be authentic and impactful.

Remember that every team is different, with its own unique nuances and dynamics. Treat them as such. No cookie-cutter approach is allowed. Allow proactive feedback to serve as your team's greatest enabler for continuous improvement.

Take the time to remind someone of how and what they can be doing better. Learn from them. Don't complicate the process of constructive feedback. Feedback is two-way communication.

5. **Acknowledge and Reward** - With proactive feedback comes acknowledgement and reward. People love recognition, but are most appreciative of respect. Take the time to give your teammates the proper accolades they have earned and deserve. I have seen too many leaders take performance for granted because they don't believe that one should be rewarded for "doing their job."

At a time when people want to feel as if they are making a difference, be a thoughtful leader and reassure your team that you are paying attention to their efforts. Being genuine in your recognition and respect goes a long way towards building loyalty and trust. It organically ignites extra effort!

When people are acknowledged, their work brings them greater satisfaction and becomes more purposeful.

6. **Always Celebrate Success** - At a time when uncertainty is being dealt with each day, you must take the time to celebrate success. This goes beyond acknowledgment – this is about taking a step-back and reflecting on what you have accomplished and what you have learned throughout the journey.

   In today's fast-paced, rapidly changing world of work, people are not taking enough time to understand why they were successful and how their success reverberated and positively impacted those around them. I have seen leaders fall into the trap of self-aggrandizement – because of what their teams accomplished – rather than celebrating the success stories that in many cases required tremendous effort, sacrifice and perseverance.

   Celebration is a short-lived activity. Don't ignore it. Take the time to live in the moment and remember what allowed you to cross the finish line.

Leaders are only as successful as their teams and the great ones know that with the right team dynamics, decisions and diverse personalities, everyone wins in the end.

Grading "Getting Along with Others"

In early elementary school especially, children are often graded on their ability to get along with other students and adults. So what does it mean when a child receives a grade of E (Excellent), S (Satisfactory), N (Needs Improvement), or U (Unsatisfactory) and why should a parent pay close attention to this nonacademic grade for their child?

Success in school involves being able to complete work, stay organized, cooperate with others, be positive about your own abilities, follow rules, participate in team-building and do your best work. These same attributes apply when a child grows into an adult and lives in the adult real world.

In children (and adults) think of behavior as an attempt to communicate. Since behavior is a form of communication, when your child receives a "Needs Improvement" or "Unsatisfactory" comment is he/she trying to tell adults something? Are they trying to gain attention to help solve a problem? Do they need to be able to move around more often? Are they trying to escape or avoid something – doing an assignment they don't understand?

Childhood is basically rehearsal for adulthood. Childhood is the time when children learn about the world and how to navigate it successfully. Understanding what their behavior communicates about their needs, adults can better understand how to guide the child's response.

If your child is having difficulty navigating the world of cooperating and getting along with others while they are in elementary school, this may set the stage for the same behavior as they grow to adults. And just as children must learn to cooperate with other children, so too do adults need to be able to work with others personally and professionally.

The Impact of Peer Influence, Bullying and Self-Esteem

Your 4-year-old greets you from preschool one day and announces he wants an *Ironman* lunchbox now instead of the *Superman* lunchbox he just had to have a month ago. Seems another child at school told him *Superman* isn't the coolest superhero, *Ironman* is. Your 7-year-old wants to cut her hair so she can look like her friend, Claire. Your 12-year-old pleads for the new smart phone du jour.

These are all forms of peer pressure or peer influence. A major part of your child's school experience is learning how to negotiate social relationships. This learning begins early in your child's school career. Every time your child spends time with other children they are learning from one another. It is natural for a child to want to feel accepted by his or her peers, but for some this desire can be more immense than other children, leaving them open to pressure or influence from children with a greater sense of self-confidence and less desire to fit in. The dance of negotiating social relationships and peer conflicts is a process and rarely just starts in high school.

Peer influence is when you choose to do something you wouldn't otherwise do, because you want to feel accepted and valued by your friends. It isn't just or always about doing something against your will as the term "peer pressure" denotes.

Peer influence can sometimes be positive. For example, a child may be peer influenced to try a new school activity or become more involved and dedicated to academic work. But as we know, peer influence can also be negative.

Peer influence can lead a child to conform to the behaviors, attitudes and habits of a group or clique. Sometimes being a part of a clique will lead to pressuring other kids to participate in bullying. This bullying can include everything from leaving mean notes and name-calling to sabotaging relationships with gossip, lies and rumors. Other times children feel an internal pressure to do things they think their peers are doing, they believe everyone else is doing it too. As a result, they do things they would not otherwise do with the hope of fitting in or getting attention.

Pressure to bully others often starts with a pack mentality and seems to be particularly evident online, commonly known as "cyberbullying". This can include participating in everything from online hate lists to mean social media posts. Typically, when kids cave in to peer pressure it is because they want to be liked or fit in. They fear that if they don't go along with the group or clique, then other kids might make fun of them. Because of this, bullying sometimes is an act of self-preservation. Kids are afraid if they don't exclude others, participate in gossip, spread rumors and make fun of others, then they will be the one bullied. Some kids accept the idea that "everyone's doing it" and often mistakenly rationalize that this behavior is acceptable when it is done as a group. With pack mentality, kids often leave their better judgment and common sense behind. As a result, they do not feel as much remorse as they would otherwise.

According to the website NoBullying.com each year over 3.2 million school aged students are victims of bullying, resulting in approximately 160,000 students staying home from school. (NoBullying.com, 2015) Students bullied are more likely to struggle in school, skip class, face substance abuse and commit suicide. This site also reports that suicide is the third leading cause of death among teenagers and approximately half of youth related suicides are linked to incidents of bullying and that bullying is responsible for approximately 4,400 deaths annually, and for each successful suicide among youth, there are about 100 suicide attempts. Additionally, 14% of bullying victims have considered suicide and almost 7% have actually made suicide attempts. Bullying victims who have not made suicide attempts have suffered in other ways, such as in anger, depression, anxiety, frustration, fear, embarrassment, shame, isolation, decreases in academic performance and dropping out of school. Statistics of bullying rates by gender vary. Some studies report boys are more often bullied than girls. Other studies report the opposite, that girls are bullied more often than boys. Either way the one statistic that remains constant is that bullying has spread from school hallways and bathrooms to social media. What was once an underground issue is now front and center of the bullying culture.

Bullying comes in a variety of forms, including the following: (Peck)

- **Verbal Bullying:** bullying with cruel spoken words, involves ongoing name-calling, threatening, and making disrespectful comments about someone's attributes (appearance, religion, ethnicity, disability, sexual orientation, etc.).

  - *Example:* When a child says to another child, "You're really, really fat, and so is your mom."
  - *How to Spot the Signs:* Children may withdraw, become moody, or show a change in appetite. They may tell you something hurtful that someone said about them and ask you if you think it's true.
  - *What to Do:* First, teach your kids about respect. Through your own behavior, reinforce how everyone deserves to be treated well -- thank teachers, praise friends, be kind to store employees. Stress self-respect, and help your kids to appreciate their strengths. "The best protection parents can offer is to foster their child's confidence and independence and to be willing to take action when needed," says Shane Jimerson, Ph.D., a school psychologist and professor at the University of California, Santa Barbara. Discuss and practice safe, constructive ways your child can respond to a bully. Brainstorm key phrases to say in a firm but not antagonistic tone, such as "That wasn't nice," "Leave me alone," or "Back off."

- **Physical Bullying:** bullying with aggressive physical intimidation, involves repeated hitting, kicking, tripping, blocking, pushing, and touching in unwanted and inappropriate ways.

  - *Example:* A child gets his pants pulled down on the playground at lunchtime.
  - *How to Spot the Signs:* Many children don't tell their parents when it happens, so watch for possible warning signs like unexplained cuts, scratches or bruises, missing or damaged

clothes, or frequent complaints of headaches and stomachaches.

- *What to Do:* If you suspect your child is being physically bullied, start a casual conversation -- ask what is going on at school, during lunch or recess, or on the way home. Based on the responses, ask if anyone's been mean to him. Try to keep your emotions in check. Emphasize the value of open, ongoing communication with you and with teachers or school counselors. Document the dates and times of bullying incidents, the responses from people involved, and the actions that have been taken. Do not contact the parents of the bully (or bullies) to resolve matters on your own. If your child continues to be physically hurt, and you need additional assistance beyond the school, contact local law enforcement. There are local, state, and federal anti-bullying and harassment laws that require prompt corrective action.

- **Relational Bullying:** bullying with exclusionary tactics, involves deliberately preventing someone from joining or being part of a group, whether it's at a lunch table, game, sport, or social activity.

  - *Example:* A group of girls in dance class keeps talking about a weekend sleepover and sharing pictures, treating the one uninvited child as if she were invisible.
  - *How to Spot the Signs:* Watch for mood changes, withdrawal from peer groups, and a shift toward being alone more than usual. Girls are more likely than boys to experience social exclusion, nonverbal, or emotional intimidation. The pain can be as strong as physical bullying and last even longer.
  - *What to Do:* Make it a nightly routine to talk with your kids about how their day went, advises Jennifer Cannon, a family therapist in Newport Beach, California. Help them find things that make them happy, point out their positive qualities, and make sure they know there are people who love and care about them. Focus on developing their talents and interests in music, arts, athletics, reading, and after school activities so your kids build relationships outside of school.

- **Cyberbullying:** bullying in cyberspace, involves haranguing someone by spreading mean words, lies, and false rumors through e-mails, text messages, and social media posts. Sexist, racist, and homophobic messages create a hostile atmosphere, even when not directly targeting your child.

- *Example:* When someone tweets or posts, "Billy is a total loser. Why is anyone hanging out with him? He's so gay."
- *How to Spot the Signs:* Watch to see if your child spends more time online (visiting social media pages or texting) but appears to be sad and anxious afterward. Even though he's reading painful things on his computer, tablet, or phone, this may be his only social outlet. Also take note if he has trouble sleeping, begs to stay home from school, or withdraws from activities he once loved.
- *What to Do:* Mean messages can be distributed anonymously and quickly, leading to 24/7 cyberbullying, so first establish household rules for Internet safety. Agree on age-appropriate time limits. Know the popular and potentially abusive sites, apps, and digital devices before your kids use them. Let your kids know you will be monitoring their online activities. Tell them that if they experience cyberbullying, they shouldn't engage, respond, or forward it. Instead, they should inform you so you can print out the offending messages, including the dates and times of when they were received. Report cyberbullying to the school and to the online service provider. If the cyberbullying escalates to include threats and sexually explicit messages, also contact local law enforcement.

New research is showing that the effects of bullying are not short-term and merely limited to the duration of the bullying. Instead research has shown the long-term psychological damage of bullying can last into adulthood. "Bullying is not just a harmless rite of passage or an inevitable part of growing up," said lead author William E. Copeland, PhD, a professor in the Department of Psychiatry and Behavioral Sciences at Duke University, in a study published in JAMA Psychiatry in 2013. (Copeland, Wolke, Angold, & Costello, 2013) "We were surprised at how profoundly bullying affects a person's long-term functioning. This psychological damage doesn't just go away because a person grew up and is no longer bullied. This is something that stays with them. If we can address this now, we can prevent a whole host of problems down the road." The authors of the study call for better intervention strategies, calling out the serious effects of bullying, which will hopefully "reduce human suffering and long-term health costs and provide a safer environment for children to grow up in."

So with the fact that bullying is alive and thriving in our culture, what can we as parents, coaches, educators do to help our kids navigate the unkind terrain? Interestingly more new research has identified a negative link between the classic approach of piling kids into an auditorium and lecturing them on the dangers of bullying, but a positive link between using the so-called influential or popular kids to spread an anti-conflict message and culture to their classmates. (Single, 2016) A study, which involved 24,191 students in total, was conducted by Elizabeth Levy Paluck of Princeton, Hana Shepherd of Rutgers, and Peter M. Aronow of Yale. They sought to find out what would happen if they "seeded" students at a school with anti-conflict messages and instructed them to spread those messages to their peers. "We wanted the message to come from the students themselves because of our hope that these students would change social norms of conflict," said Paluck. "Students figure out the social norms of their school, we hypothesized, by observing what other students think and do. If other students are just parroting adults, this isn't going to be a very strong signal of what they actually think. Thus, we wanted the anti-conflict messages to be sincere, to mean something to the students." The study concluded students don't really take their cues for how to behave from authority figures, but their peers. So perhaps a huge step in the right direction to effecting change in a bullying-predominant society is to enlist the help of the kids themselves, athletes included.

Specifically, here are some strategies parents can use to help their children overcome bullying. ("What Parents Can Do About Childhood Bullying," 2015)

If your child is a victim of bullying, try helping him/her with the following strategies:

Your attitude and actions

- Listen carefully to your child's reports of being bullied. Be sympathetic and take the problem seriously. Be careful not to overreact or under-react.
- Do not blame the victim. When a child finally works up the courage to report bullying, it isn't appropriate to criticize her for causing it or not handling the situation correctly. For example, don't ask, "Well, what did you do to bring it on?"
- Realize that for a child who is being bullied, home is her refuge.

Expect her to have some difficult times in dealing with victimization. Get professional help if you think your child needs it.

- Encourage your child to keep talking to you. Spend extra time with her. Provide constant support and encouragement, and tell her that you love her often!

Teach your child safety strategies

- Remember that hitting back is not a choice at school and shouldn't be encouraged. In a school with a "zero tolerance policy" for physical aggression, encouraging your child to hit back may just get him expelled.
- Encourage your child to walk away and tell an adult if he feels someone is about to hurt him.
- Talk about safe ways to act in situations that might be dangerous. For example, identify a "safe house" or store or where he can find sanctuary if pursued by bullies. Encourage him to walk with an adult or older child. Give him a telephone number of an available adult to call if he's afraid and needs help dealing with a bullying situation.
- Brainstorm and practice strategies with your child to avoid further victimization.
- Teach your child how to report bullying incidents to adults in an effective way. Adults are less likely to discount a child's report as "tattling" if the report includes:
  - What is being done to him that makes him fearful or uncomfortable
  - Who is doing it
  - What he has done to try to resolve the problem or to get the bully to quit
  - A clear explanation of what he needs from the adult (or what he wants the adult to do) to get the bully to quit.

Nurture your child's self-esteem

- Educate your child about bullying and bullies. Help her put the problem in perspective and not take it personally.
- Teach your child how to walk in a confident manner.
- If needed, help her pay particular attention to personal grooming

and social skills.

- Identify and encourage your child's talents and positive attributes; doing so may help her better assert herself among her peers.
- Encourage your child to make new friends. A new environment can provide a "new chance" for a victimized student, as she won't be subjected to the negative stereotype other classmates have of her. **Encourage her to make contact with calm and friendly students in her school.** Such action may require some assistance on your part, or perhaps a school mental health professional, to develop the child's skills at initiating contact and maintaining a friendship relationship. This is especially true if your child's learning problems make her social interactions difficult. Be sure to provide ongoing support and encouragement, because your child, due to earlier failures, will tend to give up in the face of even slight adversities.
- Encourage your child to participate in physical training or sports, even if she's reluctant. Physical exercise can result in better physical coordination and less body anxiety, which, in turn, is likely to increase self-confidence and improve peer relationships.

When should the victim's parents contact school authorities? If the bullying occurs at school, then the main responsibility for achieving this goal lies with the school officials. It's important, however, that the parents of the victim collaborate with the school to implement an agreed-upon plan for solving the problem.

If your child has been the victim of bullying at school, here are some suggestions for reporting the problem to school authorities: ("What Parents Can Do About Childhood Bullying," 2015)

- After talking to your child, but before contacting school personnel, write down the details of the bullying situations reported to you by your child. Note the dates and the names of the kids involved.
- Try to view the situation objectively and determine how serious it is.
- Your child may resist your involvement if he fears retaliation by the bully. If so, explain to your child that most bullying situations require adult intervention to resolve the problem. Let him know exactly who you plan to talk to.
- Contact school personnel for assistance in ending the bullying. First share the problem with your child's teacher(s), and work together to decide how to approach the problem. If the teacher

isn't able to get the bullying under control, go to the principal and make a formal request in writing that he or she get the bullying to stop.

- Do not contact the bully or the bully's family directly.
- Keep an ongoing log of the dates of any further bullying incidents and the actions you take to help your child deal with the bullying. Inform the school of ongoing bullying incidents.

What can the parents of the bully do? ("What Parents Can Do About Childhood Bullying," 2015)

Parents of bullies should understand that children who aggressively bully peers are at increased risk for engaging in antisocial or criminal behavior in the future. It is therefore important to try to help bullies change their negative attitudes and behavior toward others.

Your attitude and actions

- Take the problem seriously. Resist a tendency to deny the problem or to discount the seriousness of it. Avoid denial thinking such as "Boys will be boys," or "Bullying is just a natural part of growing up."
- Listen carefully and check out the facts. Do not believe everything your child tells you. Children who bully are good at manipulating adults and can be very artful at weaving a story that makes them look innocent.
- The school or the victim's parents may be documenting reports of your child's bullying behaviors. It doesn't serve your child well to deny her involvement if there is evidence to the contrary. Check out the dates and the activities and determine if there is a pattern in her bullying behavior.
- Explore the reasons for your child's negative behavior. Get professional help if necessary for your child and/or your family.

Hold the bully accountable

- Resist the tendency to blame yourself. Hold your child responsible for his own choices.
- Make it clear to your child that you take bullying seriously, and that you will not tolerate such behavior in the future. Make it clear that you expect all bullying activities to stop immediately.
- The issue of bullying should be monitored for some time through

questioning your child and regularly contacting the school to determine if his bullying behavior has stopped.

Help a bully change behavior

- Develop a clear and simple system of family rules. Offer frequent praise and reinforcement. Use non-hostile, negative consequences for violations of rule-following behavior. Consistently enforce the rules. Appropriate consequences for bullying might include the loss of privileges (e.g., television or computer game time).
- Follow through with appropriate consequences for your child's misbehavior. Do not use physical punishment, as doing so will only reinforce your child's mistaken belief that it's acceptable to bully those who are weaker to get what one wants. **If both you and the school are consistent in applying negative consequences for bullying, the chances she will change her behavior are considerably increased.**
- Spend more time with your child and monitor her activities closely. Find out who her friends are, where they spend their leisure time, and what activities they usually engage in. Is your child in "bad company"? If so, limit her exposure to the negative peer group and provide opportunities to become involved with more pro-social peers.
- Build on your child's talents and strengths, and help her develop less aggressive and more empathetic reaction patterns.
- Reward your child for positive, caring actions and for peaceful problem solving.

What can — and should — parents expect the school to do? ("What Parents Can Do About Childhood Bullying," 2015)

Whether your child is a bully, victim, or bystander, you should expect the following from his/her school:

- School administrators, teachers, and staff should take bullying problems seriously. The school should investigate the situation and let you know what steps they're taking to help stop the bullying.
- Written school policies and rules against bullying, harassment, and intimidation should be in place — and be enforced.
- Teachers and administrators should speak to the bully and his

parents. They should also tell him what the consequences will be if he doesn't stop bullying others. If the bullying continues, the school should enforce the pre-determined consequences immediately.

- Teachers and administrators should increase adult supervision in the areas of the school campus where bullying incidents are most likely to occur.
- School personnel should be well-informed about the children who are being victimized by bullies so they can monitor and provide support to the victims as needed. They should also communicate often with the victims' parents to tell them how the situation is being handled at school.

Bottom line on peer influence, bullying and self-esteem: children are always going to be influenced by their peers, it's human nature. But a culture of intolerance for bullying begins at home by modeling, teaching and expecting kindness in your child.

Just like the farmer who plants tomato seeds in July and expects tomatoes to grow when he should have planted the seeds in early spring, the parent who doesn't raise a child from infancy to be a kind, caring, confident person will not see those important characteristics in their child when they reach adulthood.

How Can Playing Sports and Being on a Team Help with Peer Pressure, Bullying and Self-Esteem?

When you join a team, you instantly become a part of an extended family and there is strength in numbers. You now have an association to a group of people who share a common bond that goes deeper than a surface connection. Playing sports encouraged me to interact and engage with like-minded peers. As I evaluate the majority of my personal relationships today, it's no shock that sports were the common denominator that brought us together. Sports are a great confidence booster. The mere fact that someone chose you to be on a team can boost confidence, self-esteem and personal image. Peer pressure is usually the result of kids seeking the approval or acceptance of others by succumbing to pressures that are more negative than positive. When children play sports they feel accepted and their confidence increases because there is a need for their talent and contribution. They become an intricate component of the team and inherit an entire new family. Sports are a great resource in helping kids learn how to set goals and execute a strategic plan. I believe team sports not only help with the maturation and personal development of student-athletes but sports also give them a since of belonging. One of the first lessons you learn about being a member of a team is, "It's one for all and all for one." When bullies know you belong to a team they have to think twice about engaging because the engagement is not one-on-one, it's the bully against the entire team.

The REason We Play Sports

RESEARCH AND RESOLUTION

> *"Nobody has ever been able to say what sport is quite. But life would hardly be the same without it. Perhaps that's because sport means a number of opposite things. It is as tangible as a golf club and as intangible as a dewy morning; exciting as a photo finish, serene as ebb tide. It is competition, composure, memory, anticipation. Sport is not all things to all people. But today it is something in more different ways to more people than it has ever been before. It is play for many and work for a few. It is what no one has to do and almost everyone wants to do. It represents, on the one hand, challenges willingly accepted - and on the other hand, gambits willingly declined. Its colors are as bright as cardinal's feathers; as soft as midnight on a mountain trail. It is as loud as a stadium at the climax of a World Series - and as quiet as snow. It is exercise and rest. It is man exuberant and man content - Sport is a wonderful world."* (Sports Illustrated , 1981)

What is it about sports that is so magical? What makes it such a powerful influence on our lives? The answers to these questions may be different for each person you ask, but every response you get will be filled with passion and be from the heart.

People have been involved with sports in one way or another since ancient times. The spirit and recognition of sports took place when the Olympic Games began in Greece. Written records describe the first Olympic Games were held in 776 B.C. But sports could possibly even date back to 17,300 years ago as cave paintings have been discovered depicting sprinting and wrestling and also in 7000 B.C. cave paintings show a wrestling match surrounded by crowds.

More modern history shows sports existing as far back as 3000 years ago when humans used sports to simulate life skills needed to survive such as hunting and fishing and armies used sport games to train for war.

More recent times have given way to the growth of further organized, formal sports, regulated by set rules and expectations of fair play. Sports are also played informally with friends for fun and camaraderie. Those who participate in sports might be highly paid professionals, Olympians, college, high school or middle school players, children in organized community leagues, adults in weekend or evening leagues or children playing in their neighborhood streets. People participate in sports in the coliseum, the dome, the stadium, the city park, the backyard, anywhere space can be found to hold enough players to forge a match.

Sports have become an important part of America's culture as well as of other cultures throughout the world. Sports pervade societies to such a degree that is has been described as a microcosm of society. In other words, sports mirror the values, structure and dynamics of a society. (Sharma, 2009)

Most lives of Americans are touched by sports in one way or another. More than three-fifths of U.S. adults, approximately 162 million people, claim some relationship to sport-related activities, including 25% who are actively engaged in sports as participants, parents of children in sports, coaches, or volunteers. (USADA, 2011) 2000 U.S. Census data showed the number of youth involved in organized sports in the United States to be estimated at more than 50 million. (U.S. Census, 2000)

Sports touch our lives in so many ways, from the 4-year-olds swinging at the batting tee to the 84-year-old swinging at the golf tee; from the athletically gifted to the Butterfinger; from the physical specimen to the physically challenged; men, women, boys, girls. Many people choose sports as a source of self-expression. Sports often help us forget about a stressful day. We get pleasure from a hard workout; we revel in achieving a goal we have set for ourselves in our training; we take great pride in watching our children participate in sports; we watch with joy and anticipation as our favorite team takes the field or court. Sports are very powerful energy!

Through sports we can express ourselves physically and emotionally. They enable us to experience the gratification of personal development and experience the enjoyment of play. Sports are also about testing oneself, learning new skills, and pursuing personal excellence. Through sports we learn about cooperation, fair play, teamwork, self-discipline, and respect for others. And sports are about competition.

Competition is a part of what makes us human. We strive to be better, stronger, faster. We set rules, invent activities, arrange contests and yearn to win. There are three characteristics that are generally agreed to as being significant components of sports: *competition* - the striving to exceed the performance of others or one's own previous performance; *physical prowess* - the importance of physical skill developed through exertion and practice; *organization* - the presence of rules to provide structure. (Berger, 1991)

Sports are based on the innate desire to move and compete against the forces of nature or with oneself or others. Life is also competitive. Sports help us prepare for the competition we face in life, the highs and lows that are part of everyday living.

Children in particular benefit from involvement in sports. It has been recently suggested that youth sports have the potential to accomplish three important objectives in children's development. (Côté, 2007) First, sport programs can provide youth with opportunities to be physically active, which in turn can lead to improved physical health. Second, youth sport programs have long been considered important to youth's psychosocial development, providing opportunities to learn important life skills such as cooperation, discipline, leadership, and self-control. Third, youth sport programs are critical for the learning of motor skills; these motor skills serve as a foundation for future national sport stars and recreational adult sport participants. A fourth can also be included, building a better society.

As to the first benefit for children, improved physical health, the research touting the importance of physical activity beginning in young children is abundant. The fitness level of children involved in sports cannot be underestimated. A review of literature by TrueSport and the U.S. Anti-Doping Agency, published in its 2012 report, "True Sport: What We Stand To Lose in Our Obsession to Win" shows the following: (USADA, 2012)

- Physical activity delays the development of chronic diseases and conditions, such as heart disease, hypertension, type 2 diabetes, obesity, and osteoporosis. Sports participation leads to higher levels of cardio-respiratory fitness, stronger muscles, lower body fat, and stronger bones. Sport participants often see immediate health benefits, such as the ability to maintain a healthy weight and reduced levels of stress.
- The incidence of obesity in children and youth has doubled over the past 25 years and will affect one-third of all children by the third grade. Sports and physical activity play an important part in helping children maintain a healthy weight.
- Adolescence signals a time when physical activity and team sports participation start to decline. However, studies show that children who play organized sports at an early age have a greater

likelihood of remaining active as teens and adults than those who do not play sports.

The second benefit of youth involvement in sports is improved psychosocial development. Longitudinal studies have shown that children and youth participating in sports, when compared to peers who do not play sports exhibit the following behaviors: (USADA, 2012)

- higher grades, expectations, and attainment
- greater personal confidence and self-esteem
- greater connections with school—that is, greater attachment and support from adults
- stronger peer relationships
- more academically oriented friends
- greater family attachment and more frequent interactions with parents
- more restraint in avoiding risky behavior
- greater involvement in volunteer work
- improved attention and better information processing, storage and retrieval
- higher attention levels in the classroom
- enhanced creativity and memory, better mood, improved problem-solving abilities

There is an old saying that sports both build and reveal character. Sports at their best can promote the virtues of honesty, respect, selfless teamwork, dedication, and commitment to a greater cause. Seligman and Peterson (Peterson & Seligman, 2004) in collaboration with social scientists and youth development experts created a framework, "Character Strengths and Virtues". The framework includes virtues or core characteristics that have been valued by all societies throughout history as critical components of "good character". According to Seligman, these character strengths have been shown to be highly predictive indicators of success and a reliable path to the "good life", a life that was not just happy but meaningful and fulfilling. The virtues include: *Wisdom & Knowledge* (creativity, curiosity, open-mindedness, love of learning, perspective); *Courage* (bravery, persistence, integrity, vitality); *Humanity* (love, kindness, social intelligence); *Justice* (citizenship, fairness, leadership); *Temperance* (forgiveness and mercy, humility, prudence, self-regulation); *Transcendence* (appreciation of beauty, excellence, gratitude, hope, humor, spirituality).

Participation in sports is a fertile ground to cultivate each of these character strengths. In any given sports event, practice session, training workout, most if not all of these virtues are in play – think about the knowledge one must use to become proficient at a sport: think of the persistence, bravery, integrity one must possess to train hard; think of the social intelligence one must exhibit with fellow teammates and opponents; think of the self-regulation one must show in the heat of competition; think of the excellence and hope one focuses on as they work to perfect their sport! All of these virtues can be practiced and cultivated in the arena of sports.

The third objective in children's development is that youth sport programs are critical for the learning of motor skills. Children are programmed to move, even before birth. Movement is biologically imperative and tied to survival instinct and healthy human development.

Researchers recognize four phases of motor development: reflexive, rudimentary, fundamental, and specialized. These stages should ultimately culminate in the collective stage of possessing motor control and movement competence. Just as children need an environment in which to develop and practice academic literacy, so too do they need an environment to practice and develop "physical literacy". The concept of physical literacy is defined by the Aspen Institute's Project Play as *the ability, confidence, and desire to be physically active for life.*" (Aspen Institute, 2015) *Ability* refers to competency in basic movement skills and overall fitness that allows individuals to engage in a variety of games and activities. This outcome is achieved through a mix of informal play and intentional teaching of movement skills. (Malina, 2012)

Confidence is knowing you have the ability to play a sport and enjoy physical activity. This confidence comes for the support and encouragement from parents, guardians, coaches, teammates, and peers throughout the developmental process.

Desire is the intrinsic joy and enthusiasm for physical activity whether it is organized, unstructured, in traditional sports or for-fun play. Desire is achieved through early positive experiences that are enjoyable and motivate children to do their best.

Performance in sports is based upon children successfully maturing through the stages of motor development. And as such, sports contribute to a child's essential task of preparing their bodies for life long physical activity and fitness.

A fourth benefit of sports for children is the notion of building a better society that is more community-oriented and respectful of others through sports participation. Some research has shown that sports contributes to the development of social capital.

Longitudinal studies have found that men at age 32 who played high school sports were paid 31% higher wages than men who had not played sports. (Barron, Ewing, & Waddell, 2001) Athletic competition might serve as an excellent training ground for individuals who are already highly motivated to succeed.

Research has also shown the longer youth play sports, the greater attachment they have to their community. Studies by Eccles and Barber (Eccles & Barber, 1999) show that youth sports participation is positively related to adult involvement in community activities that can last a lifetime. Youth who participate in sports are more likely to make friends, including those of different races. (Sheets, 2005) Young athletes are better able to acquire emotional control, learn the value of teamwork, and exhibit initiative (Larson, Hansen, & Moneta, 2006), all social skills that can contribute to a better community.

There is no question that providing sports for youth to play has community benefit, if for no other reason than a child's idle time can be filled with healthy, positive activities. Lessons learned playing sports transcend the playing field, spill over into the classroom, the business world and the community. They contribute to the shaping of character and culture of our citizens. Playing sports instill "a sense of confidence, usefulness, belonging, and influence." (Boys & Girls Clubs of America. , n.d.)

People of all ages play sports for different reasons – because it is fun, because competing against well-matched opponents is exhilarating, because the relationships formed with teammates and coaches is valuable, because the feeling of personal accomplishment by pushing one's physical and emotional limits is rewarding, or because the after effects of physical exertion feel good. Whatever the reason, true sports – that is, sports played hard, fair and clean – foster personal growth and social goods. (USADA, 2012) Sports bring people together in a way not seen in other life arenas. They impart valuable life skills and tools and provide unique and profound experiences to those who participate. It is no doubt one of our most treasured pastimes and endeavors.

To sum it up in a few words, the REason we play sports is: *Sports add quality to our lives.*

The REsponsibility — MENTOR LEVEL

Testimony

Gina Luna on her son, Tyson Luna:

Happy Labor Day! Wanted you to know that you are so powerful as a role model. I am in Seattle with Tyson this weekend. We had an amazing conversation over dinner last night. He was telling me about his goals and the kind of person he wants to be. His exact words..."I want to be like Bo Porter - where I am successful and I can use my success to give other people opportunities. I respect that more than just being a really amazing athlete or businessman. You have to do good for others or you waste your talents.
Music to a mother's ears. THANK YOU for modeling the way!!!

CHAPTER 4: SPORTS PARENTING

"Behind every successful athlete is an exhausted parent." --
Unknown

Parenting a student-athlete can be extremely difficult for some, because as parents we always want what is best for our child. A parent feels an emotional connection with their child that is hard to match. That's why Tony Dungy's quote, "The best soup is made at home", has always resonated to the core of my character. Many parents struggle with being that strong force their child needs, to not only grow and mature in sports, but more importantly to grow and mature in life.

Some of the names used to describe parents can range from: helicopter parent (they hover over the child and everyone involved), mommy / daddy ball (they have one set of standards for their child and a different standard for everyone else), tunnel vision (they only see two things, their child and the child who replaces their child), and finally but surely not the least is the parent living vicariously through their child.

When it comes to raising a child, yes it takes a village because your child will interact with other adults throughout his or her development stages. The impact of the other chosen adults who will become a member of your village will heavily depend on the rearing your child receives at home. It is extremely hard to outgrow your fundamental teaching. So I'll add one important fact to Tony Dungy's great quote, "The best soup is made at home...and so is the worst soup!"

> *That is why God allowed parents to continue to age and be older than their children, to provide wisdom to the offspring. The Bible says, "Train up a child in the way he should go even when he is old he will not depart from it." PROVERBS 22:6*

> *"Whoever spares the rod hates his son, but he who loves him diligent to discipline him." PROVERBS 13:24*

Both of those scriptures remind me of my upbringing and the discipline my mom instilled in me at an early age. At times I would sit in my room and cry because I didn't understand why my mom wouldn't just let me slide. Especially when the behavior wasn't anything close to the behavior of the other children in the neighborhood.

The one story that comes to mind happened when I was a junior in high school. It was basketball season and the second semester grades came out before winter recess. I had earned all A's and B's the first semester but was late turning in an English term paper and my English grade dropped from a B to a C. My mother was not happy! After reviewing my report card, she asked what had happened with my English grade. I told her I turned in my term paper late but I was going to complete some extra credit after the break and bring the grade back up. Her response was the equivalent of having my guts pulled out of my stomach. My mom said, "Well, I don't think basketball and English are working for you, so you won't be playing in the Christmas tournament." My coach came to the house and tried to explain to my mom that I had the best grades on the team. My mother's response was, "I'm not their parent, I'm Bo's mom and he won't be playing until he brings up his English grade." Well because it was the winter break I could not complete the extra work until after the Christmas tournament. This was a painful lesson to learn and I cried for days.

Quote from Bo's mother, Beverly Porter:

"I found out his grade had dropped from a B to C," she recalled. "I don't know exactly what the reason was, maybe he rushed through a paper or whatever, but I saw that grade and I said, 'You won't be playing basketball ball' and (he said) 'But Ma, it's the Christmas tournament.' Well, you should have thought about that when you were writing your paper and when you decided to go from a B to a C."

"I told him one day you will thank me," she remembers. "I said, 'I know you're upset. I know you don't understand why. But as a parent, when you become one you'll understand and one day you'll look back on this day and thank me, but I have to do this. Does it hurt? Yes, but I know it's the right thing to do.'"

That was a lesson that helped pave the way for a disciplined Bo Porter.

Fast forward from 1988 to 2015. I want to share a text exchange from one of my high school teammates. I must say this text exchange brought tears to my eyes.

High School Teammate: Bo, I heard you were in town.

Bo: Yes. I'm here for the Newark Athletic Hall of Fame Dinner tonight.

High School Teammate: Nice. I thought you were already in the hall.

Bo: Yes, I'm in already! I'm here as the Keynote Speaker and to present scholarships.

High School Teammate: Okay. They asked me to come down. Are you in and out?

Bo: I'm in today! Out tomorrow! I start World Series coverage for the Network tomorrow.

High School Teammate: Would it have been a problem if I had asked for 2 tickets during the season? I know everyone is asking!

Bo: That's fine brother!! I'll always take care of you.

High School Teammate: Thanks in advance. Speak well tonight! Just wish my mom had pushed harder on my academics like your mom did with you. Congratulations, Porter. Love you much brother!

This text exchange immediately took me back to that cold winter night in December when my mom didn't allow me to play in the Christmas tournament. Unlike the tears I cried my sophomore year of high school, these were tears of joy running down my face. I called my mom and told her about the text exchange and thanked her for giving me the most valuable life lesson - *discipline.*

Here are a few short messages and valuable life lessons that parents should make sure are served in the soup eaten at home. The blessing of these messages will always be near and dear to my heart because of the person who gifted the transformational book and the person who wrote the book. It was Christmas 2011 and my wife gave me Tony Dungy's book *The One Year Uncommon Life Daily Challenge.* (Dungy & Whitaker, 2011) It changed my life and the lives of many others as well. Tony Dungy's book inspired me to start a spiritual book club in January of 2012. The daily book club messages were a combination of the daily message from *Uncommon Life* and my own personal additions. What started as a group of twenty people quickly grew and the daily spiritual messages were reaching over 1,800 people by 2014. I was so inspired by the impact the book club messages were having on my life, I decided to write and publish my own Daily Devotional in 2015 titled *REal Life EMPOWERED.* Tony Dungy, thank you for being a vessel for God's Kingdom and paying your blessings forward. As you read these messages that originated in *The One Year Uncommon Life Daily Challenge,* I want to remind you of one important fact about parenting and leading: you say more by what you do, than you ever do by what you say because actions speak louder than words.

Living Wisely and Prayerfully: Parents Teach Your Student-Athlete The Power Of God's Word and Prayer

What does it mean to "live wisely"? Other Bible versions translate the Greek phrase as "be self-controlled." God's truths are timeless and not gender specific. Whether you are a man or woman, maintaining a core of self-control will set you on a path toward developing other basic qualities that are key to living an uncommon and significant life: keys that focus on character, honesty, and integrity; the priorities of family and friends; embracing your full potential and mission; and living a life of faith and influence. All are designed with the intention of helping you to grow in the wisdom of God's plan for you and to live out His purpose fully.

How is your self-control? Strong in some areas, weak in others? Strive to strengthen the weak areas and remain disciplined in the strong areas. Seek God in prayer and ask Him to strengthen you where you are weak and give thanks to Him for the areas where you are strong.

Wisdom is found in reading God's word daily. It is a matter of discipline and self-control. Learning the power of prayer is a major key to heightening your impact for God's Kingdom. Remember discipline is not what you do to someone, "discipline is what you do for someone." Feeding your body God's word daily is the best form of discipline and a cup of soup that should be eaten at home daily.

Humble Soup: Parents Teach Your Student-Athlete To Be Humble

"Humility is not thinking less of yourself, it's thinking of yourself less." –Unknown

There are two kinds of people in this world: he or she who is humble, and he or she who will soon be humbled. Which one are you? Striving to be humble is the sign of a person seeking God. Those unwilling to humble themselves usually have a big ego. And EGO is an acronym for: Edging God Out!

"Those that exalt themselves will be humbled, and those who humble themselves will be exalted." MATTHEW 23:12

How often have we seen someone blowing his own horn - or trying to

- only to have it blow up in his face. This type of behavior happens in sports often. There is the player and/or coach who brag before the game about a sure victory only to play or coach the worst game ever. Or the player who showboats with the intention to bring attention to himself, "Look at me everybody."

Former University of Texas football coach Darrell Royal said, "Act like you've been there before."

Have you caught yourself saying or doing something with an intentional "look at me" attitude? It can happen to anyone. And so can falling flat on your face and eating humble pie. I'm all for showing your emotions, because I realize it's part of the game. But we can show more respect for our sport and our opponent if we implement Coach Royal's motto and express humility. And at the same time we can give the honor and glory to God.

If there is something we wish to pat ourselves on the back for it's okay to do it privately. We should also share our great feat with God and thank Him for His grace and blessings. Striving to remain humble is the sign of a person seeking God.

Let's all strive to eat *Humble Soup*!

Knowing True Balance: Parents Make Sure Your Student-Athlete Understands Time and Money

One way to determine what is important to a person is to examine two areas: time and money. Where we spend our money and how we spend our time indicate our priorities. The way we prioritize demonstrates a great deal about our relationship with God and our family. We should aim to prioritize our time and money in a way that receives approval from God and our family. My inability to manage my time effectively prior to completing *The End Game* was discussed in great length in the beginning of the book in the "Acknowledgements" section to my wife and son. I gained valuable wisdom throughout that entire process and my apology was received with love by Stacey and Bryce.

> *"Teach us to make the most of our time, so that we may grow in wisdom." PSALM 90: 12*

There is no doubt that God wants us to use the platform we have been given in a way that impacts others for Christ. Our platform can be very challenging at times because of the amount of time we spend away from our families. And for those of us with kids, who will be going out into the world soon to impact others with their own platforms (whatever those may be) our children need us as they find their way.

Sometimes striking the appropriate balance between work and family is difficult. More often, however, it is achieved with small changes, like taking your kids to school and picking them up, having lunch with your kids at school, and don't forget Mommy and Daddy need their time as well. So having a planned date night, working out together, or just time alone without the kids, is priceless. A daily phone schedule, if you are away, gives everyone something to look forward to as well as planned family vacations and/or surprise family outings whenever free time is available.

We must honor our family because the things we honor indicate where our priorities lie. How is your balance? Spend time each day evaluating how you demonstrate your priorities by reflecting on how you spend your time and money.

Showing Up: Parents Your Presence Is Priceless To Your Student-Athlete

> "Jesus returned to the Sea of Galilee and climbed a hill and set down. A vast crowd brought to him people who were lame, blind, crippled, those who couldn't speak, and many others. They laid them before Jesus, and he healed them all."
> MATTHEW 15: 29-30

Woody Allen is quoted as saying, "Eighty percent of success in life is just showing up." I think that is an overstatement because a lot would be riding on that other twenty percent. But there is a truth in that saying that I totally agree with - "Showing Up!"

"Showing Up" is something we all can do for our family and friends. You would be surprised to know how important showing up is for our children. You never know what you might miss when you are not there - a baby tooth falling out, a word spoken for the first time, the look of excitement after winning a big game or getting an "A" on a test - small miracles, but miracles everyone can see together.

Spend time with your family and loved ones for no reason at all but to be there. You will witness miracles you might otherwise miss forever.

Choose Your Words Well: Parent Be Aware Of How You Communicate With Your Student-Athlete

> "We all make mistakes. For if we could control our tongues,

we would be perfect and could also control ourselves in every other way." JAMES 3:2

I don't know about you, but controlling my tongue is quite a task and something that I've worked extremely hard to do. I first took a hard look at when, where and why did I lose control of my tongue? What I discovered was my choice of words, in-season and off-season, where very different. Why? Well, clubhouses and baseball fields seem to be particularly rife with verbal bashing, breeding grounds for sarcasm and biting words. Players, coaches, or staff try to rationalize such remarks by telling ourselves that we wouldn't say those things in other settings. The danger is that saying careless words is habit-forming. These unguarded moments become patterns for normal interaction with others. And it's tough to break the habit, to flip the switch, based on the setting.

"If you claim to be religious but don't control your tongue, you are just fooling yourself, and your religion is worthless."
JAMES 1:26

Our words matter to God. Godly people know that we cannot have a double standard of speaking one way in church and another way on the job or in the community. Our words show what kind of person we are. I used to be careless in my speech and quick to yell, especially when I was in-season. But after identifying this short coming, I petitioned God in prayer and asked for his guidance in my quest to clean up my words, regardless of the setting. I now can honestly say that my thoughts are much clearer and my actions, reactions and interactions with everyone I encounter has greatly improved.

Watch your words. What might seem harmless or funny in one setting may be completely inappropriate in another, and probably isn't harmless or funny in the first place.

When Expectations Detail Dreams: Parents Allow Your Student-Athlete To Discover Their Passion

"Don't copy the behavior and customs of this world, but let God transform you into a new person by changing the way you think. Then you will learn to know God's will for you, which is good and pleasing and perfect." ROMANS 12:2

It is considered normal for young children to aspire to be like their parents. When my son, Bryce, was four years old his teacher asked,

"What do you want to be when you grow up?" At the time, Bryce's answer was no surprise to me. He said, "I want to be a Major League Baseball player just like my daddy." Now is baseball Bryce's passion or is that because he is witnessing how passionate I am about baseball?

We see this all the time. Children aspiring to be doctors, lawyers, artists, professional sports players, CEOs, presidents or police officers. Sometimes these plans are the children's plans, but often they are really their parents' plans. But as they get older, children confess to no longer having those dreams. They learned to conform to the expectation of those around them. Many of us go through life trying to play a role expected of us by parents, spouses, or society itself.

Fast forward four years and the 8-year-old Bryce has found his passion and it's not baseball! Is he good at baseball? Yes! Bryce likes baseball but he LOVES basketball! Bryce's answer to that same question is still no surprise to me because I witnessed the transformation. "Bryce, what do you want to be when you grow up?" "Daddy, I want to practice law and play NBA basketball."

Expectation is good. Motivation from others can be great. But at the end of the day DESIRE is what really counts. Someone else can light your fire, but YOU better have your own gasoline and wood to keep that fire burning.

God put certain things in your heart, passion and dreams that others don't have. If your dreams develop in the process of seeking God's will and fit within His overall purposes, follow them. He would not have given them to you if they were not important. Parents, this does not mean we should not encourage our children to be professional sports players, doctors, artists, lawyers, CEOs or professors. We should continue to be a great example of what PASSION and DESIRE in any field can accomplish and with prayer and faith, believe that your children or people who you are blessed to influence, develop and use those same traits, PASSION and DESIRE, to be successful in whatever professional career path they choose.

God made you the unique person you are. Discover your passion. Dare to dream, to reach, and to soar. The world needs what you have to offer.

The Benefits of Discipline: Parents Discipline and Allow Your Student-Athlete To Be Disciplined

"Uncoachable kids become unemployable adults. Let your kids

get used to someone being tough on them. It's life, get over it."
--Pat Murphy, Alabama Softball

What is discipline? Why is discipline important for all? One of the common myths about discipline is that discipline is something you do to someone. No, discipline is what you do for someone.

> *"Endure hardship as discipline; God is treating you as sons. For what son is not disciplined by his father?" HEBREWS 12:7*

Discipline should be obvious to any of you who are parents or in some position of authority with others who look to you for direction or guidance. Without discipline and consequences for the violation of standards, you would be stuck trying to reason with little satisfaction or opportunity to change the behavior. Otherwise chaos ensues; behavior potentially worsens as they continue to defy the standards.

It may be painful at times when the Lord directs us to discipline, but as He shows us when He disciplines us, it is necessary for their health and well-being. In the same way, it's no fun when the Lord disciplines us, but He's doing it for our good. Actions have consequences. Just like a parent teaches a child, our Father teaches us.

> *"Our fathers discipline us for a little while as they thought best; but God disciplines us for our good, that we may share in his holiness." HEBREWS 12: 10*

What True Love Looks Like: Parents Love Your Student-Athlete Unconditionally

I tell my son Bryce all the time, "I just love watching you play." What if God only loved us when we did right, and cast us aside whenever we did wrong? It would be extremely hard to trust our relationship with Him. But that's not the case because God's love for us is unconditional.

> *"So I now am giving you a new commandment: Love each other. Just as I have loved you, you should love each other. Your love for one another will prove to the world that you are my disciples." JOHN 13: 34-35*

Love is a commitment and a way of acting, not necessarily a feeling. Love is an act of spiritual maturity, based on the eternal significance of each person and of what God is doing in our life. Looking through the dark lenses of this world clouded by sin and suffering, it doesn't always make sense now, for example, to forgive someone who has wounded you deeply or hurt others. But we have God's assurance that when you follow the way of love, you are walking in the way of life.

> "Love is patient and kind. Love is not jealous or boastful or proud or rude. Love does not demand its own way. Love is not irritable, and it keeps no record of when it has been wronged. It is never glad about injustice but rejoices whenever the truth wins out. Love never gives up, never loses faith, is always hopeful, and endures through every circumstance." 1 CORINTHIANS 13: 4-7

Being a Christian comes with certain expectations, and one of them is that we will love others. Our Christian conduct is proof as to whether we love each other and loving each other is proof that we belong to Christ.

> "If we love each other, God lives in us, and his love has been brought to full expression through us." 1 JOHN 4: 12

Loving others is the best soup in the world! Make sure it is being served in your home daily!

CHAPTER 5: PRINCIPLES AND VALUES OF EDUCATING STUDENT-ATHLETES

"Someday their playing time will end and they need to have a strong education foundation to continue to grow and thrive in the workplace. The skills learned in sports like dedication, persistence and constant improvement will be very helpful in the classroom. Likewise, the thinking skills learned in the classroom will help them in their athletic endeavors." --Linda Wawrzyniak, President of Higher Standards Academy

Discipline is something I learned at a very young age. My mother was a strict disciplinarian who kept a close eye on my schoolwork. Balancing sports and education is something parents can do but they must be serious and realistic about it.

"Sports is a career with a timeline but your education will last forever." --Beverly Porter

In June of 1993 I received the call that the majority of little league kids dream about. It was the first week of June and I was home in New Jersey for a short summer break before heading back to University of Iowa for the second semester of summer school. With hopes of being drafted in baseball at the end of my junior year, I had attended summer school after my freshman and sophomore years. Many of the Midwest area scouts were unsure about my desire to sign because I was always forthcoming about my strong desire to graduate before entertaining any thoughts about signing professionally. Due to my commitment the previous two summers, I was year away from graduation. So if the draft came calling, I was in an excellent position to weigh all of my options.

Well, my childhood dream of being drafted came true that hot and sunny day in June of 1993. I wasn't home at the time of the call but received a message to call the Chicago Cubs. As I reflect back on that day, I remember almost feeling like I was in a dream. With family gathered in the living room at 793 South 14th Street, I returned the call. The next five minutes of the conversation happened so fast in my mind that it is hard to recall the exact detail. Someone answered and I said,

"Hello. This is Bo Porter from the University of Iowa. I received a message to call this number." The representative from the Cubs said, "Bo, congratulations, you have just been drafted by the Chicago Cubs." I immediately starting crying. I was completely overwhelmed with joy and had tears running down my face. I handed the phone to my mother and she continued the conversation. The Cubs said that I would receive a contract offer by certified mail the next day and a scout would be in touch to discuss getting me signed.

The Cubs' letter arrived the next day and to my surprise the contact offer was unsatisfactory as it related to the financial offer. After some long discussions with my mother, Coach Hicks, Coach Banks (Head Baseball Coach at Iowa), Hayden Fry (Head Football Coach at Iowa) and Coach Elliott (my Defensive Back Coach at Iowa) I decided not to sign!

As only faith would have it, one of the most well-known and respected scouts in baseball was Ed Ford. Ed was the Chicago Cubs National Cross Checker and he lived in New Jersey. So Ed remembered scouting me as a high school player three years before. Like any great scout, Ed called the Scouting Director of the Chicago Cubs Al Goldis to check on the status of my situation. Al informed Ed that the offer was too low and I was headed back to Iowa for my senior season. Ed asked Al if he minded if he conducted a private workout with me. Al said, "Sure, let me know how it goes". Ed called to set up the workout in Bayonne, NJ. Well, let's just say the workout went great and I broke another window, but this time it wasn't in the church parking lot! It was a house that was set beyond the left field fence at the field in Bayonne. After the workout Ed called Al Goldis and said, "We need to sign this kid!" Al was in nearby Geneva, NY getting ready for Opening Day for the Chicago Cubs New York Penn League, Geneva Cubs. Ed called later that night and asked if I would be available to head up to Geneva to meet Al Goldis and workout with the team for a few days. I agreed and the next day I was in the car with Ed Ford headed to Geneva. After two days working out in front of Al Goldis and the Geneva coaching staff, I sat down with Al and Ed to discuss the possibility of getting a deal done. With contract negotiations reopening, I again discussed the revised offers with my group of advisors. After weeks of back and forth we finally agreed to terms and I was officially a member of the Chicago Cubs.

One of the main topics during the negotiations was my mother's unwillingness to allow me to sign any contract that would prohibit me from graduating from the University of Iowa during the Fall of 1994. She was also interested in who would be responsible for paying for my full scholarship, which I would lose once I sign a professional contract. Al Goldis and Ed Ford assured my mother and me that the MLB Scholarship Fund would pick up full payment of my scholarship. Then came the tough part of the negotiation. Because I injured my shoulder and red-shirted in football my freshman year, I still had two more years of football eligibility. By then It was late July and football practice was set to start the first week of August. The contractual agreement allowed me to attend Iowa during the fall semester of 1993 and play my junior year of football. I would then report to Spring Training during the spring semester of 1994 and play baseball through the month of July and return to Iowa for the fall semester and my senior year of football. With all systems a go, I was motivated more than ever to make the most of this incredible opportunity.

Over the next two years, I realized how behind I was compared to the rest of the baseball players. After being drafted in June 1993 and not playing that summer due to the length of time it took to negotiate my contract, I had lost a lot of preparation time. So once the football season ended in 1993, I focused all my energy on preparing for the 1994 Spring Training.

I reported to Spring Training in Mesa, Arizona in the best baseball shape of my life. I was excited and at the same time unsure of what to expect. I finished the 1994 season playing for the Peoria Chiefs in the Midwest League. That summer everything started coming together and the organization took notice. With football set to start the first week of August in Iowa City, I was being asked about my desire to return for my senior year of football. There were two reasons I had to return to Iowa, the first being the commitment I made to my mother before signing my professional contract. I promised my mother that I would graduate. The second was the commitment I made to Coach Elliott, the University of Iowa and my teammates. True commitment is "the ability to carry out your commitment long after the mood in which you made the commitment has passed." So, I returned to Iowa for my senior year, was named All-Big Ten, team Defensive MVP and graduated with a degree in Communications Studies. I was now armed with a degree, a professional baseball contract and a projected NFL draft pick.

When asked about Bo Porter, Bob Elliott, University of Notre Dame Special Assistant to the Head Coach, said, "He grew up in a tough circumstance and because of that and because of his mother-- I give a lot of credit to her for a lot of that-- he had a vision and was way beyond the kids that come out of environments like that and he was a good student because of that."

Simply The Best!

The day legendary Coach Pat Summitt passed away I posted the following on my social media pages:

> *Pat Summitt was a Hall of Famer and a true ambassador for all sports. She championed women everywhere and created opportunities for them. Would there be a WNBA without her incredible influence? I don't think so! There's no question, [she] was really one of the greatest coaches of any sport. Pat was so much more than a Hall of Fame coach; she was a mother, mentor, transformational leader, philanthropist, humanitarian and inspiration to so many. Her legacy will live on through the countless people she touched throughout her career. Rest in peace, Pat. My thoughts and prayers are with her family. May God's grace comfort them during this time of mourning and beyond! #ALegacy #SimplyTheBest*

Summitt was widely regarded as one of the toughest coaches in college basketball history, men's or women's, and was well known for giving her players an icy stare. She ran an elite women's basketball program in Knoxville for nearly four decades, with a record of 1,098-208 (.840 Winning Percentage) which includes the most victories in the history of NCAA Basketball when she retired. Under Summitt the Lady Vols won eight NCAA titles, along with 32 regular-season and SEC tournament championships. Tennessee appeared in the NCAA Tournament 31 times and boasted 14 Olympic team members, 34 WNBA players, 21 All-Americans and 39 All-SEC players.

Pat Summitt's basketball accomplishments are astonishing and may never be matched. I never played for her but I can only imagine how that stare would make her players feel. After researching the career of Pat Summitt, I now realize she gave her student-athletes and this world so much more than a stare. One of Pat Summitt's best quotes says it all, "The world isn't a place you live, it's a place you aspire to impact. What have you done to leave your mark and impact in the space you occupy in this world."

Well, how about this for impacting the space she occupied? Beyond the athletic success, all of Pat Summitt's players who completed their eligibility in Knoxville graduated from Tennessee. It was her players that Summitt valued most, making sure all 161 of them graduated. Now that's inspiring, impactful and what I call transformational leadership.

Here's what future NFL Hall of Famer and former Tennessee Volunteer Payton Manning had to say about Pat Summitt, "Pat was a great friend to me, a great resource, and even though I never played for her I always felt like she was kind of one of my coaches. I used to lean on her for advice. She was one of the people who I spoke with my junior year in college when I was deciding whether to turn pro or stay for my senior year, and she gave me some invaluable advice."

After her passing I spent weeks researching Pat Summitt and I only wish I could have played for her. What an amazing woman! As I read the countless stories of her life, her accomplishments on the court are only an introduction to who and what Pat Summitt was all about. What is always mentioned is the impact she had on lives, whether they played for her, against her, or never met her at all. We know the women's game is what it is because of her, but there are so many other ways she touched lives.

To Sum It Up:

Here is a letter shared by Pat Summitt's friend, co-author and Washington Post columnist Sally Jenkins. The letter was written to former player Shelia Collins some 34 years ago but will speak to the character of Pat Summitt.

Summitt's letter to Shelia Collins dated November 22, 1982:

Shelia,

This is your first game. I hope you win for your sake, not mine. Because winning's nice. It's a good feeling. Like the whole world is yours. But it passes, this feeling. And what lasts is what you've learned. And what you've learned about is - life. That's what sport is all about - life!

The whole thing is played out in an afternoon. The happiness of life, the miseries, the joys, the heartbreaks. There's no telling what will turn up. There's no telling how you'll do. You might be a hero. Or you might be absolutely nothing.

There's just no telling. Too much depends on chance, on how the ball bounces.

I'm not talking about the game. I'm talking about life. But it's life that the game is all about. Just as I said, every game is life, and life is a game. A serious one. Dead serious. But here's what you do with serious things. You do your best. You take what comes.

You take what comes and you run with it.

Winning is fun .?.?. Sure.

But winning is not the point.

Wanting to win is the point.

Not giving up is the point.

Never letting up is the point.

Never being satisfied with what you've done is the point.

The game is never over. No matter what the scoreboard reads, or what the referee says, it doesn't end when you come off the court.

The secret of the game is in doing your best. To persist and endure, "to strive, to seek, to find, and not to yield."

I'm proud to be your Coach,
Pat Head Summitt

There is a Chinese proverb: "When planning for a year, plant corn. When planning for a decade, plant trees. When planning for a life, train and educate people." Everyone can learn from the life of Pat Summitt. Winning on the court and field will always have its place in the record books. But winning in the classroom and setting a high standard of academic achievement will continue to yield a return for society long after the last game is won. Pat Summitt will never add to her personal win total of 1,098 but because she properly watered and nurtured her fruit, they will continue to harvest and add to her legacy. So in essence the NCAA basketball's winningest coach will never stop winning...Pat Summitt is **Simply The Best!**

CHAPTER 6: PRINCIPLES AND VALUES OF COACHING AND LEADERSHIP

"A coach will impact more young people in the year than the average person does in a lifetime." --Billy Graham

When asked to define a coach, legendary Dallas Cowboys Coach Tom Landry may have defined it best, "A coach is someone who tells you what you don't want to hear, who has you see what you don't want to see, so you can be who you have always known you could be." Parents, the three most important decisions in your life will be choosing your faith, choosing your life partner and choosing who to entrust the responsibility of coaching your kids.

The Selection of a Coach

The selection of a coach for your child is such an important decision because the parent is allowing the coach to share in the personal development of their most beloved and prized possession, their child. The decision of who will be responsible in this personal development can mean the difference in your child's overall well-being and success in life. The decision should be based upon these factors: 1) is the coach a transactional leader - meaning the coaching style is one in which the coach instructs your child from a supervisory role. This leader promotes compliance through both rewards and punishments; or 2) do you want a coach who believes in transformational leadership - a coach who creates a vision to guide the change through inspiration and encourages others to raise one another to higher levels of morality and motivation. Who can best help your child be the best performer not only on the field but off the field is the most important decision you will make in the personal development of your child.

In the eyes of a kid, coaches are viewed very much like parents and/ or teachers and whether the coach knows it or not their relationship plays a major role in a kid's confidence and self-esteem. Every notable athlete at some point has been asked to recognize those who have impacted their athletic career and in doing so they typically recognize an educator or coach. As a former athlete, parent of an athlete and now coaching athletes, I know first-hand the impact teachers and coaches had on my career and the role we play as coaches. My number one goal as a coach is to help each player reach his or her potential.

My First Coach

When I joined the South Ward Little League Dodgers, I was blessed to have a coach named James Miller. Mr. Miller was an avid sports fan, but more importantly, he was a New York Yankees fan. As a Yankees fan Mr. Miller was accustomed to first class everything and he demanded that of his ball players. My introduction to the importance of professionalism in appearance came by way of a lesson from Mr. Miller one day before one of my Little League games.

I showed up on a Saturday morning with my uniform unwashed and dirty from the night before. Mr. Miller pulled me aside and asked, "What team are you playing on today?" As a confused 9-year-old, I looked him in the eye and said, "The Dodgers." Mr. Miller then looked at me and said, "Not with that uniform." Holding back tears, embarrassed and ashamed I didn't know what to say. We didn't have a washer and dryer at home, my mother had worked late at her second job that night so did not have a chance to wash my things and neither did I have time to wash my uniform the night before.

Lucky for me I had a caring coach. Mr. Miller went to the trunk of his car, pulled out a clean pair of pants and a clean jersey. He took my dirty uniform and with a kind smile said to me, "This is what a uniform looks like."

This was my introduction to the importance of professionalism in appearance as it relates to sports. I was blessed and lucky enough to have a coach who cared enough to not only explain but to also provide an answer for a problem for which a 9-year-old child did not have the answer. Sometimes a coach's greatest impact happens during teachable moments.

Leadership Research

Having witnessed first-hand, researched and studied the topic of leadership, I have discovered the twelve traits that an authentic leader needs to possess and execute daily in order to effectively lead. These are the twelve absolutes that truly successful leaders are able to master, from sports executives and coaches, to businessmen, and past presidents.

"Before you are a leader, success is all about growing yourself. When you become a leader, success is all about growing others." --Jack Welch

Here are "The Twelve Traits of An Authentic Leader":

- **Duplicate Themselves** – *Leave a legacy!* They live in the hearts of the people around them, so they never die. Success is wonderful, but significance is even better. You were made to contribute and to leave a mark on people around you. In failing to live from this frame of reference, you betray yourself. Authentic leaders are constantly building their legacies by adding deep value to everyone that they deal with and leaving the world a better place in the process.

- **Competent** – *Knowledgeable, competent, prepared!* In order for the team to follow the coach or leader, the players or people have to have complete confidence in the leader's competence to lead them. To be an effective leader, one must be extremely competent. A competent leader understands his product whether that product is a team, a church ministry, or family relationships - and they constantly strive to improve that product. Competent leaders are committed to continuing their personal growth. A competent leader is focused on constantly increasing the level of his or her competence. They understand the need for lifelong learning. Continual education is a key to effective leadership because no one can know everything there is to know.

- **Composure** – *Stand strong during adverse times!* They don't panic! All organizations, teams or businesses encounter problems on their way to success. Organizations and teams that make it through tough times, to become successful, usually have leaders who can communicate optimism to their followers. When problems arise, a good leader approaches those problems with assurance, cheerfulness, and an optimistic attitude. An optimistic attitude will inspire a leader's followers.

- **Visionary** – *Greatness starts in our imagination.* They can see it! It's real! Einstein said, "Imagination is more important than knowledge." It is from our imaginations that great things are born. Authentic leaders dare to dream impossible dreams. They see what everyone else sees and then dream up new possibilities. A vision is more than a set of goals. A leader may set goals and quotas, but that is not the vision. A true vision of the leader gives the team more than just a target. It gives the team a mission – a reason for being enthused and motivated. All leaders and teams have the ability to set goals, but great leaders and great teams are driven by a vision…a true sense of mission and purpose.

- **Enthusiastic** – *High energy, passionate, self-motivated!* Others feed off their presence. Motivating a group of individuals is not an easy task. That is why the coaches who are most successful are the ones who can motivate. The coach's level of excitement will be emulated by his or her players. It's virtually impossible to motivate others if they don't witness your level of enthusiasm.
- **Strong Self-Relationship** – *Authentic leaders know themselves and take care of themselves.* The job of the leader is to go deep. Authentic leaders know themselves intimately. They nurture a strong self-relationship. They know their weaknesses and play to their strengths. And they always spend a lot of time transcending their fears. Taking care of your physical dimension is a sign of self-respect. You can't do great things at work if you don't feel good. Authentic leaders eat well, exercise, and care for the temples that are their bodies. They spend time in nature, drink plenty of water, and get regular massages so that physically they are operating at first-class levels of performance.
- **Courageous** – *Willing to take the road less traveled and doing not what is easy, but WHAT IS RIGHT!* It takes a lot of courage to go against the crowd. It takes a lot of courage to be a visionary. It takes a lot of inner strength to do what you think is right even though it may not be easy. We live in a world where so many people walk the path of least resistance. Authentic leadership is all about taking the road less traveled and doing not what is easy, but what is right.
- **Rich Morals** – *High standards, authentic, believer, character.* Walk the talk & talk the walk! Who you are speaks far more loudly than anything you could ever say. Strength of character is true power - and people can feel it a mile away. Authentic leaders work on their character. They walk their talk and are aligned with their core values. No human being is perfect. Every single one of us is a work in progress. Authentic leaders commit themselves to excellence in everything that they do. They are noble and good. And in doing so, people trust, respect, and listen to them. They are constantly pushing the envelope and raising their standards. They do not seek perfection and have the wisdom to know the difference. What would your life look like if you raised your standards well beyond what anyone could ever imagine of you?
- **Emotional Intelligence** – *What to say, when to say it and who to say it*

to. They will take one for the team! One of the primary things that people are looking for in their work/life experience is a sense of emotional sensitivity. Authentic leaders create workplaces that foster human linkage and lasting friendships. They realize it's about the people and the people feel valued.

- **Great Communication Skills** – *Well-spoken in all sectors.* Delivery is a major strength! Excellent listener! Communication is not a one-way street. It is not just about speaking to people; it requires the speaker to listen and get feedback. Whenever a leader communicates, they must not only talk, but they must also listen. Having a vision is important, but it is useless if the leader cannot communicate that vision to his team. The task of the leader is to communicate clearly and repeatedly the organization's vision, strategy, goals, and objectives, and to communicate its values, mission purpose, and principles. The leader has to sell his vision to his players…not as 'my vision for this team", but as "our vision for success". This is true whether you are selling a baseball team on a new strategy, or a nation on a new policy.

- **Compassionate Servant Heart** – *First and foremost a good leader serves others.* True leadership is not about being the boss. It is about being a servant. Lead from the heart. They care about people. View themselves as equals. Committed. ALL IN! Leadership is about people. The best leaders wear their hearts on their sleeves and are not afraid to show their vulnerability. They genuinely care about other people and spend their days developing the people around them. They are like the sun: the sun gives away all it has to the plants and the trees. But in return, the plants and the trees always grow toward the sun.

- **Truthful** – *Leaders speak their truth.* They are clear, honest, consistent, responsible and willing to be vulnerable! They don't say things to please others and look good in front of the crowd. Authentic leaders are different…They consistently talk truth. They would never betray themselves by using words that are not aligned with who they are. Speaking truth is simply about being clear, being honest, and being authentic.

Before studying this topic, I looked at leadership as a very broad concept that was hard to define. After studying and learning about leadership, I have found that it is actually something comprehensible, once the characteristics of a leader have been identified. Remember, being an authentic leader is a continuous effort to learn, grow and adapt. Those blessed to occupy the space of leadership are priceless commodities to the people they serve. I hope your reading of the twelve traits of an authentic leader will help transform and transcend you and those you're blessed to lead, to even greater heights.

The REsponsibility of All Parties In Sports and How They Impact the Development of Those Playing Sports

RESEARCH AND RESOLUTION

The idiom, "it takes a village to raise a child" is no truer than in the development of a child who plays sports. A cadre of entities all contribute to the positive and yes, negative outcomes of this development for youth. Some who impact the development of those playing sports are parents, coaches, educators and community members. And as in Newton's Third Law of Motion, for every action there is an equal and opposite reaction; what one entity does to affect development (positive or negative) of a child playing a sport, that action has consequences for the other entities.

Positive Youth Development

Before one can address the responsibilities and impact of those who live and work with student-athletes, a little background in positive youth development must be reviewed. There are many definitions of optimal youth development among researchers. Hamilton suggests, "Optimal development in youth enables individuals to lead a healthy, satisfying, and productive life, as youth and later as adults, because they gain the competence to earn a living, to engage in civic activities, to nurture others, and to participate in social relations and cultural activities. (Youth) can actively shape their own development through the choices they make and interpretations they place on their experiences." (Hamilton, Hamilton, & Pittman, 2004)

It has been written that through optimal youth development, "good youth" emerge. "Good youth are said to experience more positive than negative affect, to be satisfied with their life as it has been lived, to recognize what they do well and use their strengths to fulfill pursuits, and to be contributing members of society." (Fraser-Thomas, Cote, & Deakin, 2005)

Development is a process not a goal. Children, adolescents and adults continue to develop throughout their lifetimes. Therefore, promoting youth development is never finally achieved and should be continually sought to progress. John Dewey in 1938 referred to this notion by stating that the purpose of development is to enable a person to continue to develop. (Dewey, 1938)

A framework of critical components of positive youth development is found in Lerner et al.'s five desired outcomes of youth development, the five "C's": (Lerner, Fisher, & Weinberg, 2000)

- **Competence** – knowledge, skills and behaviors that enable a person to function more effectively to understand and act on the environment. Enables a person to accomplish what he or she intends.
- **Character** – what makes a person intend to do what is right, just and good.
- **Connection** – social relations with adults, peers and younger children.
- **Confidence** – the assuredness a person needs to act effectively. Enables a person to build and demonstrate competence and character in challenging situations.
- **Caring/Compassion** – a sense of sympathy and empathy for others.

Collectively, these processes will lead to the sixth "C" of positive youth development: Contribution. As physically, socially, psychologically, emotionally, and intellectually healthy youth develop into adults, they will choose to contribute or "give back" to civil society, and in doing so, be promoting the positive development of the next generation of youth. (Fraser-Thomas, Cote, & Deakin, 2005)

Positive Youth Outcomes Through Sports

Youth sports have the potential to accomplish many positive developmental outcomes. Not only can sports build better athletes, but it can also build better people. The National Research Council and Institute of Medicine (NRCIM) (National Research Council and Institute of Medicine , 2002) has outlined four main areas of youth development: physical, psychological/emotional, social, and intellectual. The process of optimal youth development and the process of optimal development of youth in sports mirror one another. For a child to be successful and happy playing sports they must progress through and achieve the same positive human qualities they need to develop into successful, happy adults.

The following is a summary of how the four main areas of positive youth development, as outlined by NRCIM, can be applied to positive youth development within the framework of sport.

- **Physical development** - Physical activity is essential for a child's optimal growth and development. Research shows physical activity helps control weight, builds lean muscle, reduces fat, contributes to a healthy functioning cardiovascular system, hormonal regulatory system and immune system, promotes improved muscular strength and endurance, flexibility, muscle and joint development, decreases risk of obesity and adolescents involved in physical activity are less likely to smoke. (USADA, 2012) Athletics also help children understand and adopt healthy lifestyles at an early age that continues throughout their lives.

- **Psychological/emotional development** - Participation in sports has been shown to have many positive effects on the psychological and emotional development of children. Some of these effects include higher self-esteem, stress reduction, opportunities for challenge, fun, enjoyment, and an overall increase in life satisfaction. Children involved in sports learn about determination, organizational skills, responsible risk-taking, and accountability. Additional research shows that youth who are highly involved in sports are more "psychologically resilient", that is, better able to recover from problems. (USADA, 2012)

- **Social development** - Research has shown that involvement in structured sport activities fosters positive social development in children. Among the findings are increased social success, positive peer relationships, improved leadership skills, greater adult career achievement, lowered school dropout rates and delinquent behavior, and development of social skills such as cooperation, assertion, responsibility, empathy, and self-control. (Fraser-Thomas, Cote, & Deakin, 2005) Sports provide children with the opportunity to engage in positive relationships with adults, which is especially important when such relationships are not available at home. Sports participation also helps build character by learning to navigate between right and wrong and learning valuable life lessons that they can carry with them throughout their life.

- **Intellectual development** - Numerous research studies have shown a positive correlation between sports participation and intellectual development. High school sports involvement in particular has been positively linked with school grades, school attendance, choosing demanding courses, time spent on homework, educational aspirations during and after high school, and college attendance. (Marsh, 1993) (Snyder & Spreitzer, 1990), , (Eccles & Barber, 1999) (Whitley, 1999) CDC research (CDC, 2010) has concluded that physical movement can affect the brain's physiology by increasing cerebral capillary growth, blood flow, oxygenation, production of neurotrophins, growth of nerve cells in the hippocampus, neurotransmitter levels, development of nerve connections, density of neural network, and brain tissue volume which in turn may be associated with improved attention; improved information processing, storage and retrieval; enhanced coping; and enhanced positive affect.

Negative Youth Outcomes Through Sports

While most sports provide positive outcomes for youth development, research suggests that sometimes experiences are less positive.

- **Physical development** - Involvement in youth sports has been linked to negative physical outcomes such as sport-related injuries often caused by overtraining, risk-taking and the physical nature of playing a sport. Eating disorders are also becoming a prevalent health problem in children, particularly girls, who participate in sports. (Beals & Manore, 1994)
- **Psychological/emotional development** - A new and expanding area of attention in youth sports is the area of negative emotional and psychological outcomes in children who are involved in sports. Excessive pressure to win, feelings of poor abilities, and pressure to specialize too early in one sport have led youth to experience low self-esteem, low self-confidence and athletic burnout.
- **Social development** - Youth sports settings have become increasingly competitive. This coupled with the physical nature of sports, increased parental and coach aggression in the sports environment has lead youth sports involvement to be linked to numerous negative social development outcomes. Acts of violence and aggression towards opposing players, referees and even teammates have become more common in youth sports settings. Poor sportsmanship and sports aggression have increasingly become acceptable within the youth sports environment along with a decline in exhibiting positive character traits.

Features of Youth Sports Programs That Promote Positive Youth Development

Based on youth sports research, the following are suggestions for how youth sports programs can be structured to optimize positive youth development: (Holt, 2008)

- Sports programs for children (i.e. age 6–12) should include interactions between children, and between children and adults, that are based on play and opportunities to try out different forms of sporting activities. 'Sampling' and 'playing' during childhood are the primary mechanism for continued sports participation at a recreational or elite level.
- Sports programs during adolescence (i.e. age 13+) can change to be built upon more specific training activities and specialization in one sport. Adolescents should have the opportunity to either choose to specialize in their favorite sport or continue in sport at a recreational level.
- The developmental assets of the person (i.e. child or adolescent) involved in a sports program should be a priority of coaches, parents, and adults involved in the sports experience. Development assets are defined as external (the positive experiences a young person receives from their world such as family support, adult role models, parent involvement, creative activities) and internal (characteristics and behaviors that help young people make thoughtful and good choices and prepare them for challenges to their inner strength and confidence).
- The eight setting features of the National Research Council Institute of Medicine (National Research Council and Institute of Medicine , 2002) should be implemented in sport programs to provide youth with a context that promotes developmental assets and the growth of life skills, competency, and responsibility. The eight setting features include:
  - Physical and psychological safety – refers to the existence of safe and healthy facilities and practices that encourage secure and respectful peer interactions in order to build confidence in youth and allow them to enjoy participation in sport.
  - Appropriate structure - refers to existence of clear and consistent expectations of rules and boundaries, focusing on deliberate play during childhood and transitioning to

deliberate practice during adolescence.

- Supportive relationships – relates to strong support, positive communication and connectedness, especially by coaches. Training coaches about basic principles of positive youth development is likely to result in better youth sport programs and sporting environments that promote a child's competence, enjoyment and motivation as well as psychological, social, and physical growth.

- Opportunities to belong – highlights the importance of inclusion and building a sense of belonging, team unity and cohesion.

- Positive social norms – refers to the development of values and morals such as fair play, sportsmanship, cooperation, responsibility, empathy, and self-control.

- Support of efficacy and mattering – focuses on the importance of programs that are child-centered, and promote empowerment and autonomy to choose their level of involvement in a sport and provide opportunities to experience challenges.

- Opportunities for skill-building – emphasizes the importance of providing opportunities for learning experiences and skill-building through developmentally appropriate program designs and coaching.

- Integration of family, school, and community efforts – refers to the importance of programs that integrate family, school and community to create optimal environments for increasing communication and lessening conflicts.

- Youth sports programs must be designed in consideration of children's healthy development over time. Administrators, coaches, and parents must look beyond the next game or the season finale, to focus as well on the long-term positive developmental outcomes of the child-athlete. In 2005 Canadian Sport For Life (CS4L) was founded to provide developmental guidelines for coaches, parents, educators and community organizations involved in youth sports. To accomplish this goal, they developed the Long-term Athletic Development Model (LTAD). LTAD focuses on developmental rather than chronological age and correlates athlete development with their physical and psychological growth as opposed to their growth in calendar years. (O'Sullivan, 2014) There are seven stages within the basic LTAD model: (Canadian Sport For Life)

- Stage 1: Active Start (0-6 years)
- Stage 2: FUNdamental (girls 6-8, boys 6-9)
- Stage 3: Learn to Train (girls 8-11, boys 9-12)
- Stage 4: Train to Train (girls 11-15, boys 12-16)
- Stage 5: Train to Compete (girls 15-21, boys 16-23)
- Stage 6: Train to Win (girls 18+, boys 19+)
- Stage 7: Active for Life (any age participant)

Stages 1, 2 and 3 develop physical literacy before puberty so children have the basic skills to be active for life. Physical literacy also provides the foundation for those who choose to pursue elite training in one sport or activity after age 12. Stages 4, 5 and 6 provide elite training for those who want to specialize in one sport and compete at the highest level, maximizing the physical, mental and emotional development of each athlete. Stage 7 is about staying Active for Life through lifelong participation in competitive or recreational sport or physical activity.

- The role of coaches and parents in sport is more than simply promoting motor skill development. Parents and coaches have a significant impact on the personal and social development of children involved in sport. Given the importance of these relationships, appropriate training that includes the principles of positive youth development should be provided to all adult leaders in youth sport programs.

Features of Youth Sports Programs That Negatively Impact Youth Development

While certainly most, if not all parents, coaches, educators or community representatives never set out to purposely damage or hinder the development of a child in sports, often it happens through the actions of the adults involved in the program. The following are features of a sports program that are in fact detrimental to the positive development of a child: (National Research Council and Institute of Medicine , 2002)

- Structure where physical and health dangers are present
- Verbal abuse

- Communications that instill fear and insecurity
- Chaotic, disorganized autocratic structure
- Age inappropriate training
- Relationships which are cold, distant, over-controlling, focused only on winning
- Behaviors resulting in exclusion, marginalization, favoritism
- Norms that encourage violence or cheating, disrespect for others
- Practices that undermine motivation and desire to learn, are unchallenging and have an excessive focus on winning
- Practices that promote overtraining, injuries, bad physical and intellectual habits, undermine school and learning and offer no opportunities to learn physical, psychological, and social skills
- Structure where discordance, lack of communication and conflict exist

Responsibilities of Parents, Coaches, Educators and Community

As stated earlier, it takes a village to raise children who are both high-performing and happy. It takes consciously guiding a child to follow their own path and become what they are capable of becoming. A life involved in sports should be fun for the child and bring enjoyment into their lives. And enjoyment in sports doesn't just come from winning; it comes from having control, gaining competence, having a sense of purpose through participation in sports, connecting with adults and peers, learning compassion, and internalizing character traits.

The responsibilities of parents, coaches, educators, and community members for positive development of youth playing sports are interdependent – all entities must be on the same page, work from the same playbook, give consistent, parallel messages and actions for youth to gain optimal development.

These responsibilities can be demonstrated through the framework of five desired outcomes of youth development, the 5 C's: Competence, Character, Connection, Confidence, Caring/Compassion and through the framework of NRCIM's four main areas of youth development: physical, intellectual, psychological/emotional, and social.

Parents' Responsibility

- Be patient, understand that sports, like school, requires a long and difficult learning process

- Learn about normal, healthy child development
- Understand factors affecting sports performance
- Be consistent in your actions and expectations
- Allow your children to fail and remind them of the lessons learned from failing
- Teach your child to succeed by overcoming failure
- Praise the effort instead of the outcome
- Teach the positives that sports bring to their lives
- Ensure that your child's coaches are qualified to guide your child through the sport experience
- Allow your child to be coached by the qualified persons you have identified
- Develop a partnership with your child's coach, understand your role as the parent, not parent/coach
- Listen to your child actively, respect their feelings and opinions, make an effort to understand what your child is trying to express
- Teach your child to express gratitude towards teammates, coaches and officials, model this yourself as well
- Keep a balance between sports, school, family life, spiritual life
- Provide a safe environment for your child, both physically, emotionally and developmentally
- Teach your child that success in sports isn't just about winning; it's about the progress of development, as a person and an athlete
- Help your child set performance goals, not the outcome goal of winning
- Be willing to progress from a leadership role during your child's early sport participation to a following and supportive role during later adolescence
- Model good sportsmanship for your child, always
- Make your actions match your words and intentions
- Teach your child to resolve conflicts peacefully and with consideration of the other's perspective
- Help your child learn and apply life lessons
- Hold your child's coaches, educators, schools and community to the same expectations you have of yourself towards positive development of your child athlete
- Teach your child to play competitively, but with humility and to win and lose with dignity
- Be aware of your actions and reactions to positive and negative

outcomes
- When you are certain your child is in a safe environment, "Release your child to the game" (Brown) let the sports belong to them, be supportive, but remember their accomplishments belong to them
- Be in the most important role for your child – their biggest fan, not coach, not referee

Coaches' Responsibility

- Understand the stages of child development, understand children
- Understand factors affecting sports performance
- Coach from a position of sound long term athletic development, for example, LTAD
- Provide a safe environment physically, emotionally and developmentally
- Model character and values in practice and games
- Treat each child with respect and fairness
- Instill a love of sports and a passion for achievement – not just winning
- Conduct sports programs based on youth developmental stages, in appropriate settings and those which foster the developmental assets (external and internal discussed previously)
- Be willing to listen to children, value their opinion
- Believe that with encouragement, guidance and practice children can make good decisions
- Teach and model to play competitively, but with humility and to win and lose with dignity
- Coach with awareness for teaching life lessons while at the same time teaching athletic skill
- Be consistent in your actions and expectations

Educators' Responsibility

- Hold your student-athlete responsible for their academic performance
- Believe that the student-athlete is just that – student first, then athlete
- Expect your student-athlete to work equally as hard in their academics as their athletics
- Be consistent in your actions and expectations

- Educate from a solid understanding of healthy youth development
- Understand factors affecting sports performance
- Value sports participation and its effect on positive youth development
- Recognize and value the extra effort it takes to perform academically along with athletically
- Collaborate with parents and coaches for the optimal development of the student-athlete

Community's Responsibility

- Be an information resource for athletes and their parents
- Demonstrate support for student-athletes through media, acknowledgement by individual businesses for local athletes and teams
- Encourage businesses to financially support community sports
- Understand the stages of child development, understand children
- Understand factors affecting sports performance
- Provide safe environments where children can play, learn and practice sports and hold games
- Provide education and training for coaches
- Understand and demonstrate the value of community connectedness through youth sports
- Collaborate with parents, coaches, educators for the optimal development of youth in sports
- Support youth sports despite win/loss outcomes
- Use youth sports as a way to make your community a healthier place for youth and their families to live and grow
- Provide a sports development system which based on inclusion regardless of socio-economic status, race, culture, ethnicity, or gender

Conclusion

The benefits of youth sports participation in the raising of children who become competent, confident, connected, compassionate adults with strong character are many and proven. This undertaking is best accomplished through a village of participants who understand their role and responsibilities of how they impact the development of student-athletes. Parents, coaches, educators and communities must collaborate and work in unison from a framework of proven youth development features to ensure the optimal positive development of children who play sports.

The REality — GRADUATE LEVEL

Testimony

Joshua LeBlanc:

The fall of 1997, I met a man that started out as my coach, but would later become a mentor and close friend. He would teach me things through the game of baseball that would help shape me into the man I am today. This man was Bo Porter. I learned quickly that baseball was a passion of Bo's, but philanthropy was equally as important. Bo was able to draw so many parallels from the sport of baseball to everyday life. Many lessons that I still carry with me to this day like, "Life is like a bank account, you get out of it what you put into it. So if you come up short there is only one person to point the finger at, and that is you." Bo's tutelage has taught me that there is a formula to success. It is: hours of hard work, tons of sacrifice, diligence, and you have to have a strong foundation of family and faith. With that blueprint I have been able to go from that little scrawny and raw overlooked kid, to a college graduate, a 2004 sixth round selection of the LA Angels of Anaheim, obtain my MBA, and now a financial coach and a mentor to the youth in my community. Thank you Bo for allowing me to see what you saw in me all those years ago. You have left an imprint on me that has helped me achieve feats that I never thought were possible. Your intellect and altruism are a huge part of the reason why I am who I am today.

CHAPTER 7: FINANCIAL LITERACY AND CAPITALISTIC ENTERPRISE

Shaquille O'Neal had an extremely successfully career playing professional basketball for 19 years. He is an NBA Hall of Famer and even before retiring he made a name for himself as a media personality and commentator. However, after Shaquille stepped off the court something incredible happened: he became a consummate businessman with a number of exciting, very profitable ventures.

During Shaquille O'Neal's long playing career, he earned an estimated $292,198,327, that's a ton of money. What is amazing is that with the way his investments and business ideas have performed, he stands to make more with his business ventures than he did playing in the NBA. Today, Shaquille O'Neal is worth over $350 million, and the number only increases each year as his business portfolio grows and reaches new heights of success.

O'Neal has been sticking his hands into various pots and reaping millions for a while now, but few people have any idea just how far his entrepreneurship goes. He has never stepped completely out of the media spotlight, but he has chosen to play it very smart with his investments and he doesn't flaunt what he is up to. Shaquille simply assesses a business idea's potential, creates a plan, and then makes it happen.

Shaquille O'Neal's business accomplishment is amazing in itself, but here is what makes it even more amazing. During an interview on "In Depth With Graham Bensinger" (Bensinger) , Shaquille revealed how he spent a million dollars one day because he lacked total knowledge of FICA and taxes. It was that experience that led a family friend to suggest the hiring of a financial advisor and to better educate himself about finances because he was in position to make a lot more than the million dollars he spent that day. So Shaquille listened to wise counsel and let's just say, the proof is in the pudding.

Money Management and the Professional Athlete

Yearly Forbes reports on the world's highest paid athletes. Here is just the top 10 for 2016: Christiano Ronaldo - $88 million; Lionel Messi -

$81.4 Million; LeBron James - $77.2 million; Roger Federer - $67.8 million; Kevin Durant - $56.2 million; Novak Djokovic - $55.8 million; Cam Newton - $53.1 Million; Phil Mickelson - $52.9 million; Jordan Spieth - $52.8 million; Kobe Bryant - $50 million.

These are top-of-their-sport athletes. Still the average run-of-the-mill pro athlete will make more in one season than most Americans make over their lifetime. But despite the mind-boggling salaries, many professional athletes wind up broke, in bankruptcy, even homeless. For example, Allen Iverson made over $200 million, filed for bankruptcy in 2012; Jose Canseco made $45 million over his career, filed for bankruptcy in 2012; Antoine Walker made over $108 million, filed bankruptcy in 2010.

For some perspective, there were 854,690 non-business bankruptcy cases in 2015. There were 124.6 million households in America in 2015. So the average household bankruptcy rate likely sits around .69% during any given year. Bankruptcy for the professional athlete is staggeringly higher and it is more common than one would think. In fact, if the data is accurate athletes lose their money at an alarming rate. According to Mint.com 60% of NBA players file bankruptcy within five years of retirement, more than 78% of NFL stars will file for bankruptcy within five years and MLB players file for bankruptcy four times more often than the average U.S. citizen.

Seven pitfalls that lead an athlete to bankruptcy are: (Crooks, 2013) (Preston, 2013)

1. Overspending

Scott Bercu, a financial accountant for professional athletes, believes athletes spend like mad, and blow their savings too rapidly. He said, "They see their salaries as infinite, like it doesn't end, like they can't spend it all. But if you get $5 million a year, by the time you get done paying your agent and taxes, you have $2 million left to spend."

2. Small window, large earnings

The average career span in the NBA, MLB and NFL is 4.8, 5.6 and 3.5 years, respectively. The longevity of financial bloom is short. Professionals in this industry have a small window to make their millions, and if they don't, they cannot survive on their savings for very long (even if they saved responsibly).

3. A lack of finance knowledge

Sports leagues are now offering seminars to help educate their athletes on personal finance, but it is still an issue many do not understand. Athletes see prominent people spending money, and they believe that their spending pattern should be the same. However, athletes fail to take into account that those prominent members have spent a lifetime learning about financial responsibility and budget strategies and most athletes spend their lives practicing and playing a sport.

4. Poor investment decisions

According to Ed Butowsky, managing partner of Chapwood Capital Investment Management, athletes are targets for poor investment pitches. He said, "Chronic over-allocation into real estate and bad private equity is the number one problem in terms of a financial meltdown. And I've never seen more people come to me about raising money for those kinds of deals than athletes."

5. Athletes entrust their money's management to the wrong people

The NFL Players Association claimed that 78 players lost a total of $42 million between 1999 and 2002 as a result of bad financial advisors. Bob Young, managing director for APEX Wealth Management, says athletes often don't know who manages their savings. He said that he frequently asks players how they're doing (financially), and they'll often respond, "I have no idea. All the bills are paid by someone else."

6. Real talk

Many professional athletes end up in financial trouble for a very clear reason: divorce and child-support payments. Adonal Foyle, author of the new book, Winning the *Money Game: Lessons Learned From the Financial Fouls of Pro Athletes*, writes divorce and child support are two things most young athletes never anticipate. (Foyle & Redick, 2015) "Early in my career, I heard a league official say that once they retire, there is an 87% divorce rate among NBA players," says Foyle. "Although I haven't verified this number, based on what I've witnessed, it seems about right."

And then there is the matter of pro athletes fathering multiple children with multiple women. Foyle cites "Where's Daddy?", the classic 1998 Sports Illustrated cover story that explored this phenomenon.

Shawn Kemp, then a forward for the Cleveland Cavaliers, had an on-court meltdown that year that was attributed to his stress over child-support payments: At 28, he had seven children. By age 20, former NBA player Latrell Sprewell had fathered three children by three women. The article listed NBA stars from Patrick Ewing to Larry Bird to Scottie Pippen to Jason Kidd to Stephon Marbury to Isiah Thomas as those making child-support payments on out-of-wedlock kids. "I'd say there might be more kids out of wedlock than there are players in the NBA," one top agent told the Sports Illustrated. NBA star Jason Caffey (earnings: $35 million over eight years) filed for bankruptcy in 2007, after his arrest for nonpayment of child support, which carries mandatory jail time. He has 10 children by eight women. So even though a player can choose to file bankruptcy here are two financial obligations that can never be dismissed by bankruptcy: child-support payments and taxes.

7. All in the family, friends, friends of friends, family of friends...

For many young athletes unimaginable and unfamiliar wealth is dropped into their laps when they are too young and immature to process it. "Almost none of us come from wealthy families," Foyle writes. "The vast majority of us do not even come from middle-class families. Instead, we sign multimillion-dollar contracts as 20-year-olds with little or no financial knowledge." Ex-NFL player Raghib "Rocket" Ismail described to Sports Illustrated in 2009 what it was like to sit in a meeting about his financial future as a very young, naive athlete: "I once had a meeting with JPMorgan," he said, "and it was literally like listening to Charlie Brown's teacher." Foyle also says almost never discussed is the psychology of the poor athlete suddenly made rich, and the financial demands that family and friends will almost always place on him. "When your parents come and ask you for money, or your entourage member, you know you can say 'no' — but what's the cost? Parents will say, 'We raised you; we took care of you.' Friends will say, 'I always had your back.' These people are attached to the athlete psychologically."

Adonal Foyle's sudden wealth as a professional athlete never destabilized him, and he credits his foster parents for his outlook on money. It probably helped that his dad was an economist, his mother a professor of women's studies and sociology. He says they would have conversations about what is important in life and how to be a moral person. So by his junior year in college, when he was drafted by Golden State, then three years later signing a four-year, $16 million deal Foyle says because of the conversations with his parents and the values they instilled in him he never looked at money as reflective of his value as a player or a person; it was a tool to be deferred, to work for him. "I always looked at each contract as my last," he says. He tells stories of being the sole guy in the locker room who wouldn't buy a luxury vehicle. "I didn't care what others thought of me when I drove a Toyota 4Runner my rookie year," he writes. "It was what I could afford."

Adonal Foyle learned well from his parents and his own good intuition. He was much more careful with his money than the average athlete. He never had an entourage and didn't buy things that would not help him keep and grow his wealth. He met with financial planners often and planned for the day should a career-ending injury occur, which did after 13 years in the league.

When his professional sports career ended he knew he wanted to help younger players plan for their future. "We owe it to our brotherhood — and society, too — to have this conversation, in a really raw way," Foyle says. "We all make bad decisions over the course of our career. The question is: Do we learn from it? Or do we keep doing it?"

Seems clear that lack of financial education and an even deeper lack of desire to pursue one is costing professional athletes a whole lot of their earnings. This needs to change and change now.

Sports in America is a capitalistic enterprise. We have all witnessed the negative coverage of athletes throughout the years. Media coverage has magnified the impact of these negative stories and the financial ramifications can be extremely costly to players...if they have not been properly prepared for the limelight. I have always subscribed to this model: you sign players and you invest in people.

Hall of Fame Coach Bill Parcells is one of my most valued mentors and I have had countless conversations with Bill about players and team building. During our first meeting to discuss team building Bill said, "Not every player is good for your team. There's such a thing called an NFU, 'Not For Us'. In other words, the player may be good enough to play in the league but you don't want the baggage that will accompany his presence." So whenever I'm asked about or evaluating a player, I always ask myself, "Is he for us or is he an NFU?" Without question, in sports, church, family and business, character counts and make-up matters.

In this next segment we will take a closer look at how character questions can impact the potential earning and capitalistic enterprise of an athlete.

Character Impact

It is said that a picture is worth a thousand words, but sometimes a picture might just be worth upwards of $8 million. At least this may have been the case with Laremy Tunsil and the recent 2016 NFL draft.

In early April 2016 Laremy Tunsil was considered to be in line for the number one pick, and if not first then certainly no less than sixth. But that suddenly changed when a video of Tunsil wearing a gas mask and smoking a substance from a bong surfaced minutes before the start of the draft. Seemingly upon being advised of the existence of the video, the Baltimore Ravens passed on Tunsil and took Notre Dame's Ronnie Stanley at number six. It wasn't until the thirteenth pick that the Miami Dolphins finally took Tunsil.

This drop from the top six pick positions down to the number thirteen pick in all likelihood cost Laremy Tunsil between $6.65 million and $8.03 million. If the Ravens passed on Tunsil because of the video, this one picture might have cost Tunsil as much as $8.03 million. Based on past rookie salaries the sixth round pick in the draft will sign a four-year deal worth about $20.48 million. As the thirteenth pick in the draft, Tunsil will likely only get a four-year deal worth $12.46 million. If Tunsil makes the maximum of his contract, then he will have missed out on $8.03 million.

Each player has a guaranteed amount of money in their deal. As the thirteenth pick in the draft, Tunsil's guarantee is roughly $6.65 million less than the guarantee given to the sixth pick. In the end, Tunsil will be missing out on an amount of money between $6.65 million and $8.03 million because a lapse in judgement and character was caught on video and was made public by a hacker on his Twitter account for less than 15 seconds.

In addition to the marijuana video surfacing, minutes after Tunsil was picked by Miami, an image showed up on Tunsil's Instagram account showing a text message conversation, allegedly between Ole Miss assistant athletic director John Miller and Tunsil, about paying rent and electric bills for Laremy's mother. Tunsil admitted that evening that he took cash from an Ole Miss coach.

There is still the not so small matter of the lasting implications the drug use video and alleged impropriety at Ole Miss will have on Laremy's and his alma mater. With the NFL's policy on substance abuse, Tunsil may potentially be referred to a professional drug counselor when he arrives in Miami. He may also potentially be entered into phase one of the NFL's substance abuse program, which is standard operating procedure for a new player who has had a drug-related circumstance while in college.

NFL spokesman Brian McCarthy said, "Whenever there is conduct or behavior that involves a substance of abuse, the player can be referred for evaluation and potential entry into the substances of abuse program. The determinations are made by clinical professionals. The primary objective is to provide assistance to address any issues and give the player the best opportunity to succeed in the league."

As for Tunsil's alma mater, his admission of accepting money could add to the trouble Ole Miss is already facing. Ole Miss had already been under NCAA investigation, including for past issues involving Tunsil. He was suspended for the first seven games of the 2015 season while the NCAA investigated. The school announced in October it was informed by the NCAA that Tunsil accepted extra benefits, including the use of three loaner vehicles without payment.

All of these occurrences play into the perception of Tunsil's character and ethical behavior which will play a part in his reputation as he begins his NFL career.

The happenings of the 2016 NFL draft remind one of a certain young man who began his professional football career with a not so stellar reputation…Johnny Manziel. Johnny Football. Johnny Heisman.

There were signs of trouble for Johnny even in his early days at Texas A&M University. In 2012, the summer of his redshirt freshman year, Johnny was arrested in College Station. The police report states Manziel "appeared to be so intoxicated he could not answer my questions about the incident except to tell me he wanted a ride home and was sorry." He also showed police a fake ID. He was charged with disorderly conduct, failure to identify himself and possessing a false identification card.

The arrest was a mere mention in the media and after Coach Sumlin wrote to university officials vouching for Manziel, his conduct probation was overturned and he was allowed to play football as the starting quarterback for the Aggies the fall 2012 season. Johnny went on to lead the Aggies to an 11-2 season and a win at the Cotton Bowl. At the end of his redshirt freshman year, Johnny Manziel won the Heisman Trophy and Davey O'Brien Award – making him the first freshman to ever win either award.

Controversy found Johnny again the next summer when allegations arose that he had accepted money for autographs. The NCAA reached an agreement with Texas A&M to suspend Manziel for the first half of the team's season opener game against Rice after acknowledging that Manziel did not receive any money for the autographs.

In January 2014 Johnny elected to forgo his junior year and enter the 2014 NFL draft. He was projected by many to be the third pick in the first round. Cleveland Browns drafted him twenty-second. The fall from third pick to twenty-second cost Johnny Football over $12 million, right around $12,407,560.

His career at Cleveland was riddled with on and off field strife. He was fined $12,000 early in his first NFL season for a hand gesture he made to opponents and in February 2015 he checked himself into a rehabilitation center for treatment of alcohol addiction. During his second season with the Cleveland Browns, Manziel was pulled over by police after fighting with his girlfriend in the car. No charges were filed.

Over the next year several social media appearances showed Johnny partying and missing team meetings and practices. In February 2016 Dallas police announced that they were opening a criminal investigation with a claim of domestic violence involving his ex-girlfriend. On April 24, Manziel was indicted by a Dallas grand jury on misdemeanor assault charges for the incident.

He was released by the Cleveland Browns in March 2016. He is now a free agent.

Both of these young men are examples of athletes who could benefit from the principles of "The End Game." Each of these men have been given the gift of an athletic career, but with such an esteemed career comes a need to develop and practice the attributes of education, character development, fortitude, understanding the value of teamwork and contributing toward the overall good of others, leadership, time management, the ability to perform under pressure, professionalism and a servant heart.

Understanding "The End Game" and the need for REal Excellence on and off the field when these young men were early in their student-athlete years would have given these men a solid foundation for the tumultuous times ahead.

CHAPTER 8: SPORTS MEDIA AND THE FISH BOWL

Media is defined by Dictionary.com as *"the means of communication, as radio and television, newspapers, magazines, and the Internet, that reach or influence people widely."* If you watch sports on television, then you should know that the stations on which you are watching these games are willing to pay billions of dollars for the rights to show these games on their networks. Turner Broadcasting owns TNT, a cable network that airs National Basketball Association (NBA) games throughout the year. TNT has been airing games since 1988 and has been paying $445 million per year for the rights to air these matches. This is a far cry from its first contract when it was paying $25 million a year to cover NBA games in its first two years. TNT eventually went on to pay close to $70 million a year for the rights to air NBA games after that first contract ended in 1990. The value of its contract has expanded dramatically ever since.

Fox currently pays $500 million per year for the rights to air Major League Baseball games. This is part of a $4 billion deal that will go on for eight years, reaching the end of the 2021 season. This deal allows Fox the rights to a massive amount of MLB events including the World Series, one League Championship Series, two League Division Series, the All-Star Game and a large number of Saturday afternoon games.

The amount of money being paid for the rights to broadcast sporting events has done wonders for sports. The dollar value of contracts has skyrocketed and the number of media outlets covering such events are endless. Athletes today are covered more in depth than ever before. I believe the media attention surrounding sports has helped the game grow and the viewership is plentiful, but it is a double-edged sword. Because players are so heavily praised *and* scrutinized, it can become difficult to manage, especially if you are not properly prepared.

The amount of network coverage and social media outlets that can instantaneously get information to millions of people with one click of "send" has placed a neon bright light over sports and entertainment. Because of the increase in media, it is more difficult for athletes to manage the fame and scrutiny that accompanies participating in sports. Today's athletes are scouted as early as twelve years old and there are countless publications ranking their skills and potential.

When I was twelve years old we had five local television channels and you had to wait for the evening news to find out what happened in the world of sports. Well that's not the case today. Social media has essentially turned everyone in the world into a reporter. As long as you have a smart phone and Wi-Fi, you are good to go. Press record, snap a photo, upload, type your desired post and hit send. By hitting "send" you are in essence sharing your post with billions of people using social media. If you're not convinced about the significance of social media, how about this for impact...

When Tim Tebow wore John 3:16 on his "eye black" during The 2009 National Championship game, over 92 million people looked that verse up on Google. That means over 92 million people heard the gospel that day because Tim was inspired to glorify God. I'm a believer and follower of Christ and it brought joy to my heart to see the impact Tim Tebow's desire to glorify God and this single sporting event could have on our society. Wow, the power of social media - now that's transformational! Let's take a closer look at the history and platforms of social media.

Social Media

The term social media is used to describe Internet sites in which people interact and share ideas and information about multiple topics, ergo, the social part. Interacting includes sharing not only thoughts, ideas and statements, but also media such as videos, music, and photos.

The first e-mail was sent in 1971. The two computers were sitting right next to each other. The message said "qwertyuiop." (History Of Social Networking: How It All Began!, 2016) According to an infographic from social media monitoring platform Simplify360, the "Golden Era" of social media started in 2001.

Starting in 2001, there was a constant stream of social innovation that started with the first crowdsourced encyclopedia, Wikipedia. Wikipedia was followed by Friendster, MySpace, Facebook in 2004 and Twitter in 2006. Facebook and Twitter are the two top social media platforms today with 1.71 billion users of Facebook and 320 million users of Twitter. To date there are 2.3 billion active social media users. (Smith, 2016)

The Fish Bowl

It is well known that athletes, college and professional, live in the public eye. Their existence - every play, move, outing, achievement, mess up, brush with the law - is front page news. But in our culture even when their playing days are over, they still live in a fish bowl. Just ask Lawrence Taylor and Johnny Manziel.

Lawrence Taylor is an NFL Hall of Famer. He played his entire professional career as a linebacker for the New York Giants from 1981–1993. He is considered by many to be the greatest linebacker in the history of football, and has been ranked as the greatest defensive player in league history by former players, coaches, media members, and news outlets such as the NFL Network and Sporting News.

During his 13-year football career he regularly made news on and off the field. He admitted to using drugs such as cocaine as early as his second year in the NFL, and was suspended several times by the league for failing drug tests. After his retirement in 1993 he was jailed three times for attempted drug possession.

From 1998 to 2009, Taylor lived a sober, drug-free life, but in 2009 he started having troubles in his personal life again. In late 2009 he was arrested in Florida for leaving the scene of an accident after striking another vehicle with his car. Six months later in 2010 he was arrested for having sex with a 16-year-old girl. He was charged with felony third-degree statutory rape. In 2011 he pleaded guilty to sexual misconduct with a teenaged girl and was sentenced to six years probation. Most recently in September 2016, just one day after his six months probation ended, Lawrence Taylor was arrested in Florida on a DUI charge. Had he been arrested 24 hours earlier before his probation ended, he would have violated the terms of his probation and been subject to jail time.

Johnny Manziel is also no stranger to on and off the field news coverage. In 2012 Manziel became the first freshman to win the Heisman Trophy, Manning Award, and the Davey O'Brien National Quarterback Award. He began his sophomore year at Texas A&M but his eligibility for the 2013 season was under question after reports surfaced that he had signed autographs for money. In August of 2013, the NCAA reached an agreement with Texas A&M to suspend Manziel for the first half of the team's game against Rice (the first game of the season), after acknowledging that Manziel did not receive any money for the autographs. After completing his sophomore year, he elected to leave college for the NFL draft. He was drafted by the Cleveland Browns as the 22nd overall pick of the 2014 NFL Draft.

Despite some success as a rookie player, Manziel struggled with consistency and his professional career was marred by off-field controversies. It seemed for a time Johnny Manziel was covered more by

TMZ Celebrity Gossip and Entertainment News in bars partying than by ESPN. In 2014, Manziel was indicted by a Dallas grand jury on misdemeanor assault charges stemming from an altercation with his girlfriend. Also in 2016 he was released from the Cleveland Browns and Nike severed its relationship with him. He was not signed by another team before the start of the 2016 season, but instead has returned to Texas A&M as a student to complete his degree in recreation, parks and tourism sciences. He is listed as a senior with the university.

Even if the NFL did come calling again Manziel still has a four game suspension hanging over his head for violation of the NFL's substance abuse policy. The NFL is also investigating the matter of the misdemeanor assault charges. If Manziel were to be signed by an NFL team, he could face further discipline under the league's personal conduct policy.

In both cases, the public limelight and inquiring minds have followed these men after they were no longer active professional players. And as such their reputations and judgement of their character continue to be tried in the court of public opinion.

CHAPTER 9: THE MUSIC AND POST-CAREER OPTIONALITY

Retirement Styles

In a 2009 New York Times op-ed, former professional baseball player Doug Glanville recalled one of his favorite baseball mentors telling him to fight retirement: "Never give the uniform back," the mentor urged. "Let them rip if off your body. Once you give it back...it will never be the same and neither will you." (Glanville, 2009)

No matter who the player, how great or how marginal their professional sports career, every player must face leaving the sport at some point. For some it is an abrupt pink slip far before they are ready to leave the game. For others it is at the end of a storybook career.

For those who end a long successful sports career by their choosing, there seem to be two distinct ways in which to approach their upcoming retirement. Derek Jeter, Peyton Manning, Tim Duncan and Kobe Bryant all announced their respective retirements within two years of each other from 2014 to 2016. All played their respective sports for 18 to 20 years. All four have had top-of-their-sport success. All four made the decision to retire on their own terms.

Jeter and Bryant chose one path of announcing their retirement. Manning and Duncan the other. Jeter and Bryant took the path of announcing their retirement a year in advance of the actual ending date. This meant they spent their last year playing as a yearlong celebration or farewell tour, if you will. Each game in each city was a chance to see them play one last time. Jordan Brand even launched a campaign intended "to celebrate Jeter, the mark he's left on the game, and his relationship with the (Jordan) brand," the company said in a news release. The campaign was dubbed "RE2PECT ." (Nike, 2014) Jeter wore No. 2 on his jersey.

Manning and Duncan each went down the opposite path of announcing their retirements. Manning announced his upcoming retirement on March 7, 2016, a month after he and his Denver Broncos defeated the Carolina Panthers in Super Bowl 50 saying, "There's something about 18 years, 18 is a good number, and today I retire from professional football."

It took Tim Duncan just 150 words by way of a letter posted on the San Antonio Spurs website to announce his retirement. In the end he said he chose retirement because playing the game of basketball "wasn't fun anymore".

Each of these four men had to claim which path they felt they needed to choose when announcing the end of their very distinctive careers. No one way right, nor wrong, just how each had to internalize the finishing of their sports life work.

Music and Sports

Music has always been connected to sports. When fans are asked what constitutes an enjoyable sporting event, they normally list these three, but in no particular order: good team, good food and good music.

How about this for the importance of music? MLB wanted to implement a policy in an effort to shorten the length of ML games. The "Pace of Game" policy was presented to the players and after carefully reviewing the different ways in which MLB wanted to trim time, the players responded with a resounding request that simply said, "As long as we can keep our walk up music!" Walk up music is a song selected by the player to be played over the PA system before the player's at bat. The music has essentially become a part of the game's fabric, to the point that most fans can tell you who is batting by listening to the music being played. The music also becomes a part of the player's mental psyche. So in the end, "the music" was non-negotiable. Talk about the power of music!

Throughout this book we have discussed in detail the importance of education and how a sports career will eventually come to an end. Most of us will not have the option to leave on our own terms. The length of a player's career can range based on a number of different factors. Some of those factors are controllable and others are uncontrollable. Since this is the music chapter, let's title your playing career "the music", and while the music is playing, you need to dance. What does dance mean? Dance simply means *use your platform for corporate engagement and collaboration to leverage future business endeavors*. Magic Johnson has mastered this concept and we will spotlight his accomplishments later in this chapter.

Sporting events are the number one form of business entertainment for corporations and business professionals. Having access to public figures can greatly enhance a company's image and add monetary value. Here is the reality: sports are a capitalistic enterprise and having professional athletes associated with your company's brand adds value.

Why Companies Partner with Professional Athletes for Marketing and Branding

Companies partner with celebrities, including athletes, because they often appeal to broad audiences and many demographics. Co-branding endorsements generate exposure to the brand, and from there benefits range from association to recognition followed by positive perceptions, brand loyalty and ultimately increased sales. Research abounds on why this works - why consumers buy products endorsed by athletes. Commonly cited motivators include nostalgia, knowledge of the sport and an affiliation for the buyer.

Exceptionally well-paired brands and athletes achieve vastly more impressive results because the individual athlete becomes the living embodiment of the product. Key attributes on and off the field (or pitch!) are conflated to product benefits, producing a compelling, unified brand. When companies achieve this stereo effect, consumer demand often soars because of the powerful messaging and perceived benefits (think Derek Jeter and Gillette Fusion).

Professional athletes are in a unique position because of the media attention and influence they have in society. A product can become highly marketable when represented by an influential athlete. If a company doesn't stay focused on this very real fact sometimes they make a misstep that ends up costing their company millions if not billions of dollars in revenue.

Let's revisit Nike and the huge mistake of getting complacent with Stephen Curry. Curry was originally endorsed by Nike in 2012. Clearly, as an up-and-coming star, Curry was a hot commodity, but not quite on a LeBron James or Kobe Bryant level, as he is now. Nike assumed that their momentum was hot enough for Curry to stay with them no matter what.

Nike didn't give Curry the attention he needed (a monumental risk) and as a result lost him to Under Armour in 2013. Yes, this is just one player, and what is one endorsement loss to Nike? Well, the Curry franchise is worth $14 billion...so, I would say it was a big loss.

Endorsements are a huge part of the business in sports. So remember all the lessons you learned along the way because **"Sports is an Institution of Higher Learning."** Be sure you are using the knowledge gained and the platform God has provided to pay forward your blessing.

"Leveraging your sports career platform with corporate partnerships can only be obtained by the outward production of good/exemplary behavior from the athlete, which allows us to be marketable, creditable and useful for our sport, corporate partners, social advancements and society in general." -- Stacey Porter

Regardless how long or how short your career in sports - put on your dancing shoes!

Magic Johnson

Earvin Johnson was given the nickname "Magic" by a local Lansing, Michigan sportswriter after seeing him dominate a high school basketball game in 1974. He called Johnson's play to be "just magical" and the name stuck.

Magic Johnson is known for his illustrious 13-year career in the NBA, but now 20 years after being forced to retire when he was diagnosed with the HIV virus, he is making new magic as a business powerhouse.

His business objective is simple: *to revitalize and provide quality entertainment and services to neglected, urban communities.* He started his business career with a couple of Pepsi bottling plants, then built from there into coffee shops, shopping centers and movie theaters in urban areas. Magic says he had a dream and a concrete plan. While winding through the urban centers of cities in team buses to basketball games, he saw boarded-up businesses and a lack of retail outlets. He told himself he'd help revive some of those neighborhoods when he could.

And that's where the magic of Magic came in. While other executives steered clear of urban areas, Johnson saw opportunity. His business plan was to bring established retail brands to the inner cities by tailoring them to the residents. But his focus on underserved urban markets was often a tough sell. When seeking capital investment from the CalPERS pension fund he was rejected five times before the group finally agreed the sixth time.

Magic Johnson has been able to succeed in a business world where many former athletes have failed, beginning with his partnership with Starbucks CEO Howard Schultz. Johnson saw the inner-city market as a big opportunity for someone with the knowledge to go after it. He says, "I knew that because I lived it. I just turned it into a business." So the "The Magic Touch" turned out to be taking chains with a familiar formula that played well in the suburbs, and tailoring them so they fit the customers and cultures of the inner city. When he realized there were few if any Starbucks locations in the inner cities he set to the task of meeting with Howard Schultz.

Johnson says in his meeting with the Starbucks CEO he told Schultz, "Look Howard, Latinos and black folks. We like coffee too." He showed him how his theaters were performing, and this convinced Schultz to go 50-50 with Johnson to develop a chain of urban Starbucks locations in underserved locations. But he says a few changes were needed first. "I had to take the scones out of my Starbucks and put in things like sweet potato pie and sockittome cake." He also changed the music, like playing more Michael Jackson instead of the typical millennial Starbucks sounds.

Ultimately, Johnson ended up building 105 locations, and his success in the inner city markets was good enough that in 2010, after a 12-year partnership, Starbucks bought the other half of the business from Magic Johnson Enterprises.

To date, Magic Johnson is CEO of Magic Johnson Enterprises (MJE), a billion-dollar conglomerate with a successful portfolio of national franchises, including Starbucks, Burger King, 24 Hour Fitness, Washington Mutual Home Loan Centers, AMC/Magic Johnson Movie Theatres, T.G.I. Friday's, a television network, a portion of MLB's LA Dodgers and WNBA's LA Sparks, Magic Johnson Bridgescape Academies, which help high school dropouts get diplomas and Clear Health Alliance, which helps provide health-care for HIV/AIDS patients. Magic Johnson Enterprises franchise networks serve more than 32 million consumers annually in 163 locations in 19 states across the United States.

While Magic has redefined himself as a businessman in his basketball afterlife, his new role as business mogul has done much more than make him money. In this role, Johnson brings life back to the inner-city by creating jobs. "Creating black presidents, vice presidents, general managers, managers--that has been the best part," says Johnson in a Fortune magazine article.

His accomplishments off the court have gained him the respect of many including those at Sports Illustrated. In 2014 Johnson was the second only person to be honored with Sports Illustrated's Sportsman of the Year Legacy Award. The first was Special Olympics founder Eunice Kennedy Shriver, in 2008.

Johnson was honored not only for his basketball greatness, but also for his success in philanthropy and in business, especially his support for urban communities. "To be recognized by SI with a tribute that has only been given to Eunice Kennedy Shriver, a woman who has made the world a better place for millions with intellectual disabilities, is very special and humbling," Johnson said in a statement before the ceremony.

Sports Illustrated says of Johnson, "When he retired from the NBA, Johnson's ubiquitous smile was a beacon to basketball fans the world over. It now represents much more: a life dedicated to creating opportunity for others as well as himself. Few athletes have done more with the stardom they gained between the lines of competition, which is why SI is proud to honor him with its 2014 Sportsman of the Year Legacy Award."

"I get asked if I'm trying to help minorities or make money," Johnson recently told Sports Illustrated. "My answer is: I'm trying to do both." In 2016 Magic Johnson ranked 10th on Forbes' list of The Highest-Paid Retired Athletes with estimated earnings of $18 million in 2015. And with an estimated net worth of $500 million, and with MJE worth a reported $1 billion, Johnson is one of the most successful black businessmen in the U.S. Notably, however, there are just five black CEOs in the Fortune 500, with a sixth on the way in 2015. The list includes Kenneth Frazier of Merck, Kenneth Chenault of American Express, Roger Ferguson, Jr. of TIAA-CREF, Donald Thompson of McDonald's, Ursula Burns of Xerox, and Marvin Ellison, who will take the reins of J.C. Penney next year. (Snyder B. , 2014)

It's no wonder that on the wall of his office boardroom the phrase *"We Are the Communities We Serve"* is proudly displayed. This business and life philosophy has served Magic well.

The REality of Sports and Why Education is the Ultimate Game Changer

ODDS OF MAKING IT IN THE MLB	
High School Baseball Players	474,791
High School Senior Baseball Players	135,655
NCAA Baseball Players	32,450
NCAA Freshman Baseball Players	9,271
NCAA Senior Baseball Players	7,211
NCAA Players Drafted by MLB	678
% of High School Baseball Players to NCAA	6.8%
% of NCAA Baseball Players to MLB	9.4%
% High School Baseball Players to MLB	0.50%
MLB salary minimum	$507,500
Income after Taxes (est)	$306,530
Average Length of MLB Career	5.6 years

If you are fortunate enough to be one of the 6.8% to become a NCAA baseball player, and one of the 9.4% of that group to make it to the MLB, you'll be lucky to get **FIVE** years out of it. At a minimum salary, you will not make enough to live on for the rest of your life. What is going to provide for you and your family after baseball is over?

YOUR COLLEGE EDUCATION!

Education is the ultimate game changer.

ODDS OF MAKING IT IN THE NFL

High School Football Players	1,086,627
High School Senior Football Players	310,465
NCAA Football Players	70,147
NCAA Freshman Football Players	20,042
NCAA Senior Football Players	15,588
NCAA Players Drafted by NFL	256
% of High School Baseball Players to NCAA	6.5%
% of NCAA Baseball Players to NFL	1.6%
% High School Baseball Players to NFL	0.08%
NFL salary minimum	$435,000
Income after Taxes (est)	$282,750
Average Length of NFL Career	3.5 years

If you are fortunate enough to be one of the 6.5% to become a NCAA baseball player, and one of the 1.6% of that group to make it to the NFL, you'll be lucky to get **THREE** years out of it. At a minimum salary, you will not make enough to live on for the rest of your life. What is going to provide for you and your family after baseball is over?

YOUR COLLEGE EDUCATION!

Education is the ultimate game changer.

ODDS OF MAKING IT IN THE NBA	
High School Basketball Players	538,676
High School Senior Basketball Players	153,907
NCAA Basketball Players	17,984
NCAA Freshman Basketball Players	5,138
NCAA Senior Basketball Players	3,996
NCAA Players Drafted by NBA	46
% of High School Basketball Players to NCAA	3.3%
% of NCAA Basketball Players to NBA	1.2%
% High School Basketball Players to NBA	0.03%
NBA salary minimum	$507,336
Income after Taxes (est)	$306,430
Average Length of NBA Career	4.8 years

If you are fortunate enough to be one of the 3.3% to become a NCAA basketball player, and one of the 1.2% of that group to make it to the NBA, you'll be lucky to get **FOUR** years out of it. At a minimum salary, you will not make enough to live on for the rest of your life. What is going to provide for you and your family after basketball is over?

YOUR COLLEGE EDUCATION!

Education is the ultimate game changer.

ODDS OF MAKING IT IN THE WNBA

High School Basketball Players	433,120
High School Senior Basketball Players	123,749
NCAA Basketball Players	16,186
NCAA Freshman Basketball Players	4,625
NCAA Senior Basketball Players	3,597
NCAA Players Drafted by WNBA	32
% of High School Basketball Players to NCAA	3.7%
% of NCAA Basketball Players to WNBA	0.9%
% High School Basketball Players to WNBA	0.03%
WNBA salary minimum	$38,193
Income after Taxes (est)	$32,464
Average Length of WNBA Career	3.5 years

If you are fortunate enough to be one of the 3.7% to become a NCAA basketball player, and one of the 0.9% of that group to make it to the WNBA, you'll be lucky to get **THREE** years out of it. At a minimum salary, you will not make enough to live on for the rest of your life. What is going to provide for you and your family after basketball is over?

YOUR COLLEGE EDUCATION!

Education is the ultimate game changer.

ODDS OF MAKING IT IN THE NHL

High School Hockey Players	35,198
High School Senior Hockey Players	10,057
NCAA Hockey Players	3,964
NCAA Freshman Hockey Players	1,133
NCAA Senior Hockey Players	881
NCAA Players Drafted by NHL	7
% of High School Hockey Players to NCAA	11.3%
% of NCAA Hockey Players to NHL	0.8%
% High School Hockey Players to NHL	0.07%
NHL salary minimum	$550,000
Income after Taxes (est)	$332,200
Average Length of NHL Career	5.5 years

If you are fortunate enough to be one of the 11.3% to become a NCAA basketball player, and one of the 0.8% of that group to make it to the NHL, you'll be lucky to get **FIVE** years out of it. At a minimum salary, you will not make enough to live on for the rest of your life. What is going to provide for you and your family after basketball is over?

YOUR COLLEGE EDUCATION!

Education is the ultimate game changer.

ODDS OF MAKING IT IN THE MLS

High School Soccer Players	410,982
High School Senior Soccer Players	117,423
NCAA Soccer Players	23,365
NCAA Freshman Soccer Players	6,676
NCAA Senior Soccer Players	5,192
NCAA Players Drafted by MLS	101
% of High School Soccer Players to NCAA	5.7%
% of NCAA Soccer Players to MLS	1.9%
% High School Soccer Players to MLS	0.09%
MLS salary minimum	$60,000
Income after Taxes (est)	$45,000
Average Length of MLS Career	2.5 years

If you are fortunate enough to be one of the 5.7% to become a NCAA basketball player, and one of the 1.9% of that group to make it to the NHL, you'll be lucky to get **TWO** years out of it. At a minimum salary, you will not make enough to live on for the rest of your life.

What is going to provide for you and your family after basketball is over?

YOUR COLLEGE EDUCATION!

Education is the ultimate game changer.

The Reality of Sports and Why Education is the Ultimate Game Changer

RESEARCH AND RESOLUTION

Education (n)

ed·u·ca·tion [ej-oo-key-shuhn]

1. the act or process of imparting or acquiring general knowledge, developing the powers of reasoning and judgment, and generally of preparing oneself or others intellectually for mature life.

2. the act or process of imparting or acquiring particular knowledge or skills, as for a profession.

3. a degree, level, or kind of schooling: a university education.

This is the how the word *EDUCATION* is defined by such dictionaries as Merriam-Webster and Oxford Dictionary. Notice the emphasis on the intent of education as an intellectual preparation of oneself for mature life.

There exists such a glaring paradox in the term student-athlete. One would assume that a student who is accepted into a college or university program will be put down the path which will lead them to obtaining a degree at the end of four, five, six years. NCAA president Mark Emmert says, "Academics must continue to come first across all three divisions. We need to meet students where they are to address their learning needs and provide proper academic support. Academic performance and graduation rates have increased across the country, and we want to see those numbers continue. Students should graduate from college equipped with an education that prepares them for jobs and opportunities in today's work world." This is an admirable mission and one that must be at the forefront of the student-athlete's college experience. But how well is this mission being accomplished?

Each year, the NCAA publicly announces the Graduation Success Rate (GSR) of all Division I institutions, along with a similar Division II Academic Success Rate (ASR). The graduation-rate data are based on a six-year cohort prescribed by the U.S. Department of Education. (NCAA)

In 1990 the mandatory publication of graduation rates came into effect as a consequence of the "Student Right-to-Know Act," which attempted to create an environment in which universities would become more devoted to academics and hold athletes more accountable for academic success. (Ferris, 2004) The NCAA reports the Graduation Success Rate for Division I college athletes has climbed to 86% – two points over last year and the highest rate ever. NCAA also reports the rate increases, which measure students who began college in 2008, occurred across the board in a variety of categories, including gender, ethnic minority status and sport.

On the surface this statistic looks amazing – 86% of all Division I college athletes who entered college in 2008 have graduated with college degrees. 86%. But let's dig a little deeper. It would be important to know what degrees the 86% obtained.

College isn't just about walking across a stage with a degree in your hand. It is so much more than that. Over those four, five, six years the way you grow, mature, learn and experiment with your new knowledge within your degree content and outside of the classroom is the real body of knowledge with which you come away.

So if your student-athlete satisfies the requirements for say a degree in general studies, or multidisciplinary studies, for what career will this degree prepare them at the end of a professional sports career or if a professional sports career does not play out for them? While it is easy and understandable for an 18-year-old to only see as far as next week, it is crucial to guide the student-athlete to procure a usable degree, not just any degree to say they earned a degree and added to the NCAA's GSR. There is a huge difference in *receiving a degree* and *receiving an education* necessary to get gainful employment. The student-athlete must obtain a degree and body of knowledge that will set them up for success in their post-sports life.

If you don't think there is economic value in a college education, think again. On average, a full-time, full-year worker with a Bachelor's degree can expect to earn 84% more money over a lifetime than a colleague who has no better than a high school diploma.

According to a Georgetown University Center on Education and the Workforce study (Carnevale, Strohl, & Melton) released in 2015 a bachelor's degree can be worth up to a million dollars in additional earning power over the course of one's life and the income gap between the highest-paid college majors and the lowest-paid is more than $3 million dollars, making a degree invaluable for any student. The study analyzed wages for 137 college majors to discover the economic benefit of earning an advanced degree by undergraduate major. "Not all bachelor's degrees are created equal," the report concluded. "Our report finds that different majors have different economic value. While going to college is undoubtedly a wise decision, what you take while you're there matters a lot, too. On average, as we stated, Bachelor's degree holders earn 84% more than those with a high school diploma. However, returns to majors run a wide gamut. **At the extreme, the highest earning major earns 314% more at the median than the lowest- earning major at the median.**" Among the 15 groups of college majors studied, architecture and engineering majors are paid the most and education majors are paid the least. Graduates with degrees in top-paying college majors earn $3.4 million more than those with the lowest-paying majors over a lifetime. Not surprisingly, STEM (science, technology, engineering, and mathematics) and health and business majors are the highest paid, leading to average annual wages of $37,000 or more at the entry level and an average of $65,000. Based on this data then in some ways a student's choice of college major can be almost as important as deciding to get an undergraduate degree at all.

So what does all this have to do with a student-athlete who is certain the reason he/she is in college is to play the required number of years, earn the number of credit hours necessary to fulfill the NCAA's requirements to keep a scholarship then jump when the call of professional sports comes? The answer is not complicated. Here it is in a nutshell:

- Of the 1,086,627 kids who play high school football, 0.08% will be drafted by the NFL and play for only 3.5 years.
- Of the 538,676 kids who play high school basketball, 0.03% will be drafted by the NBA and play for 4.8 years.
- Of the 474,791 kids who play high school baseball, 0.50% will be drafted by the MLB and play for 5.6 years.
- Of the 410,982 kids who play high school soccer, 0.09% will play for MLS for 2.5 years.
- Of the 35,198 kids who play high school hockey, 0.07% will play for the NHL for 5.5 years.
- Of the 433,120 girls who play high school basketball, 0.03% will play for the WNBA for 3.5 years.

So in a typical case scenario, most professional sports careers last between 2.5 years and 5.6 years. That means by age 28 most professional sports careers are over. Imagine however, your student-athlete is one of the .09 – 0.50% who do play professional sports for a time. Without the maturity and knowledge four to six years of college can instill in them, how in the world will they be equipped to responsibly manage a multimillion dollar contract that gets dropped in their lap at age 20? And without the preparation of a marketable college degree, how will the student-athlete, now grown adult, support his/herself and family when their professional sports career days are over?

Consider now the student-athlete who realizes he/she has been given a golden opportunity in the form of a college education and wishes to take full advantage of his/her four to six years on campus but lacks the preparation to function at the college level academically. In 2012 Mary Willingham, former academic advisor/reading specialist at University of North Carolina first reported that 8 to 10% of the athletes admitted on scholarships at UNC between 2005-2012 were functionally illiterate and not able to read at a high school level and that 60% read between fourth- and eighth-grade levels. In 2014 a CNN investigation found public universities across the country where many students in the basketball and football programs could read only up to an eighth-grade level. The data obtained through open records requests also showed a staggering achievement gap between college athletes and their peers at the same institution.

What classes can a student take in college who can only read on a third, fourth, fifth grade level? Closing this kind of gap for the student to be able to compete academically at the college on top of the student-athlete dedicating 30-60 hours a week to practice, travel and game playing would seem impossible. "The gap in academic preparedness between profit sport athletes and students at NCAA (Division I) institutions perpetuates educational inequality," Willingham said. "Until we acknowledge the problem, and fix it, many of our athletes, specifically men's basketball and football players are getting nothing in exchange for their special talents."

In November 2012, when Mary Willingham first spoke out about the number of student-athletes who were not able to complete college level work, she said she began to see a pattern. Some told her they had never written a paragraph or read a book. At about the sixth-grade level, dominant or "star" athletes began to be passed through classes in middle school because they were dominant athletes and thought to be crucial for a winning team. "I had students tell me that, 'My teacher told me I wasn't going to learn anyway, so what's the point?'" Willingham said.

So perhaps the place to begin is not the first day of the student-athlete's freshman fall semester. Parents, teachers, coaches and administrators must make sure each and every student-athlete is a student first. Make their student-athletes accountable for their academics first, athletics second. Get academic help for those struggling with learning disabilities and those not achieving their academic potential. Stop the age old subculture of letting an athlete slip through the system unable to read, do computations and think critically.

As a parent or guardian you must embrace the ideology that **"education is the ultimate game changer."** It is up to you to be the advocate for your student-athlete.

The REward – PLATFORM LEVEL

Testimony

Facebook posting:

Josh Jones: *One of the keys to success is to find a mentor and learn as much as you can. I remember watching him work hour after hour on the Westbury baseball field to improve his skillset, then he took the initiative to teach at Westbury to make sure we were taking care of our grades in the classroom. Fast forward to him introducing me into coaching the youth with his Texas Hawkeyes select baseball organization, while signing me to a contract with the Florida Marlins. Congratulations to one of the hardest working people I know. All of your success is well deserved and I couldn't be more proud to be a living testimony to your accomplishments. Congrats on being named the special assistant general manager of the Atlanta Braves!!!*

Bo Porter: *Josh, thank you for that heart felt message. I'm so proud of you! I can't and won't take credit for doing God's work. I'm a vessel being used for God's glory. It's an absolute joy to witness your maturation and the impact you're having in the lives of the young men in your program. Wishing you continued blessings. Remember, I'm always a phone call away.*

CHAPTER 10: DEVELOPMENTAL PRACTICES
MBA | COMMUNITY IMPACT

The measuring stick of the ultimate impact your community service will have on those you serve may never be known nor witnessed by the person whose heart led them to serve. Community impact can be achieved in many ways; I call it the three T's of giving. You can give your **time, talent** and/or **treasures**. All three T's are needed and the amount can never fully be measured because the impact is endless.

My first experience with community service happened when I was nine years old. This introduction to altruism came on my childhood block by way of a homeowner named James Tillery, though the only name I ever called him was "Mr. Taylor". Because we didn't have a baseball field in our community, we played in the church parking lot. Across from the church parking lot was the home owned by Mr. Taylor. Routinely when I was at bat, I would hit the ball over the fence and into Mr. Taylor's living room window. And each time this prompted Mr. Taylor to pay my mother a visit to discuss the repair payment of his broken window.

It was a typical day on 14th Street and we were playing our usual pick-up game of baseball in the church parking lot. Once again I hit a homerun into Mr. Taylor's window. And as always before, Mr. Taylor came to our house to speak to my mom but this time the conversation took a different turn and a bridge of opportunity was offered by a man who committed his time and treasure to serve.

Here is how the conversation went:

Mr. Taylor:	*Well, your son broke my window again.*
My Mom:	*I'm sorry but these kids have nowhere else to play. Put me on a payment plan and I'll do my best to pay you back.*
Mr. Taylor:	*You know, I sit and watch these boys play and your son is better than most all the boys. Have you ever thought about signing Bo up for Little League baseball?*
My Mom:	*No, because I'm sure Little League costs and I can't afford it.*
Mr. Taylor:	*Well, I'm sure Little League will be cheaper for you than*

	having to keep paying for these windows.
My Mom:	*Well, there's no Little League around here and I don't have a car, so how would Bo get there?*
Mr. Taylor:	*How about if I pay the $25 registration fee and agree to take Bo twice a week to Little League practices and games, will you let him play?*
My Mom:	*If you're willing to do all of that, yes, I would love for him to play.*

With that said, Mr. Taylor signed me up and I was drafted with the first pick by the South Ward Little League Dodgers, went on to win back to back championships and was named Rookie of the Year and League MVP. That same bridge has led to a life filled with great accomplishments but none greater than my wife and I starting our own foundation in 2012, The Stacey and Bo Porter SELF Foundation.

SELF is an acronym for Sports, Education, Life Skills and Faith and through the SELF Foundation we provide the resources needed to operate the afterschool program for children being raised in underprivileged and underserved communities. Our commitment to improve the facilities within those same communities has produced groundbreaking state of the art baseball fields and renovation projects that are providing the necessary resources for the children to grow. I now refer to Mr. Taylor as the *Taylor Community Service Foundation* that provided me with a bridge of opportunity. I'm forever grateful and will continue paying forward this God-given blessing.

God's Platform of Influence

We are all in an exclusive position to have lasting influence on the people in our lives.

> *"The fruit of the righteous is a tree of life, And he who wins souls is wise."* PROVERBS 11:30

God has given everyone a platform. Some of those are broad and highly visible, but others are small - or at least they seem that way. A "small" platform is huge when it impacts even one other person who goes on to impact many. God is the author of our platform and He gives us the privilege of using it to influence others. Sometimes we don't see the results of our investments in other people's lives for years to come, if at all. But everyone's platform is unique and God has a plan for it.

When Stacey and I started the Stacey and Bo Porter SELF Foundation the driving force was our desire to use the platform God has created: to impact and influence the lives of others. We will spread God's word, His grace, our faith and give thanksgiving for how God's presence impacts our life.

You may not have a foundation, but you have influence. A platform that may seem small to you can have lasting impact that you will only discover in eternity. That is why it is important to never sell your platform short. God is a master of doing big things with small beginnings. He has put you where you are and surrounded you with the people you know for a reason.

We must use our platforms. No matter how inconsequential it seems to you, it is greatly significant to God.

Why Do Corporations Get Involved in Charitable Activity?

Traditionally, companies have given to charity because:

1. It makes them look good.
2. They care about an issue / the community / etc.
3. They want the charitable tax donation.
4. Cause-related marketing has worked for them. They get to create, for example, an awareness campaign about their product/service while also getting tax benefits and community recognition.

Today, I think a better question is, "Why do – or should - corporations engage in CSR (Corporate Social Responsibility)?"

CSR is the next generation of "philanthropy" and it involves strategically embedding social, environmental or economic benefits – or a combination of them – into the company's work. It is seen as a way for companies to "do well and do good" while also building brand loyalty with the highly sought-after Millennial cohort who increasingly throw their young but mighty weight towards those businesses which give back.

A good friend James Epstein-Reeves wrote a series of articles for Forbes back in 2012 that rather beautifully addresses this subject. Below is an excerpt of his piece exploring six sound reasons why companies should be committed to CSR: (Epstein-Reeves, 2012)

"Typically, I step on top of my soapbox to declare the six business reasons why companies should embrace corporate social responsibility. Companies that "get it" are the ones that are using CSR (or sustainability as I prefer to call it) as a way to push the following business processes into the organization:

5. **Innovation** – I know, I know, it's an over-used term. Just typing the word into Amazon will bring up nearly 150,000 items. But in the context of CSR, innovation is a huge benefit to a company and society. For example, I recently watched a video of a brief talk by Geoff McDonald who is the Unilever Global VP for HR, Marketing, Communications and Sustainability. Using the "lens of sustainability" as McDonald described it, Unilever was able to innovate new products such as a hair conditioner that uses less water. Without sustainability, the company's research and development efforts possibly wouldn't have led to such a product.

6. **Cost savings** – One of the easiest places for a company to start engaging in sustainability is to use it as a way to cut costs. Whether it's using less packaging or less energy, these savings add up quickly. For example, General Mills is on a path to reduce its energy savings by 20% by 2015. According to its 2011 CSR report, after installing energy monitoring meters on several pieces of equipment at its Covington, Ga. plant, the company saved $600,000.

7. **Brand differentiation** – In the past, brand differentiation was one of the primary reasons companies embraced CSR. Companies such as Timberland were able to find their voice and incorporate the company's values into their business model. However, as CSR has become more commonplace, using it to differentiate your brand is getting harder to do. For example, the "Cola Wars" is one of the longest running rivalries in business. Coke and Pepsi are constantly looking to grab as much market share as they can from each other. Yet they are both adopting similar, although slightly different, approaches to CSR. Both Pepsi and Coke are pursuing strategies of zero net water usage. Both companies offer water bottles made from sustainable packaging as well. In the end, although neither company is necessarily going to see strong differentiation benefits, I see the diminishing returns on brand differentiation as a sign that CSR is taking hold and is not just a fad.

8. **Long-term thinking** – "The only reason we're doing sustainability is to drive the growth of Unilever," McDonald said in the video mentioned above. Indeed, CSR is an effort to look at the company's long-term interest and ensuring that the company's

future is… well… sustainable. Hence, that's why I prefer the term sustainability to CSR. It is a shift from worrying about the next fiscal quarter's financial results to the impact business decisions today have on financial (and social) results ten years from now.

9. **Customer engagement** – What's the point of doing CSR if no one knows about it? For the past few years, Walmart has established itself as a leader on environmental efforts. Yes, you read that correctly, Walmart is a leader in environmentalism. In 2008, Walmart ran an ad campaign designed to raise awareness about the environment and the product choices consumers could make. Using CSR can help you engage with your customers in new ways. Since the message is about something "good," it can often be an easier way to talk to your customers. This is an underused tool for business-to-business company communication.

10. **Employee engagement** – Along similar lines, if your own employees don't know what's going on within your organization, you're missing an opportunity. Companies like Sara Lee created a cross-functional, global Sustainability Working Team to help create a strategy for sustainability. At a more grass roots level, the Solo Cup Company created the Sustainability Action Network to activate employees in community service focused on the company's CSR priorities."

Many athletes have recognized their ability to contribute to philanthropy by forming charitable foundations. Below is a list of many such athletes who are using their platforms to have a positive influence on people and society. Thank you for your commitment to impacting others and using your platform to accomplish important work in our world.

Athletes with Foundations

BASEBALL

- Jeremy Affeldt - The Jeremy Affeldt Foundation
- Josh Beckett - The Josh Beckett Foundation
- Craig Breslow - Strike Three Foundation
- Ryan Dempster - Dempster Family Foundation
- Curtis Granderson - Grand Kids Foundation
- Cole Hamels - The Hamels Foundation
- Tim Hudson - Hudson Family Foundation
- Derek Jeter - Turn 2 Foundation

- Josh Lindblom - The Josh Lindblom Foundation
- Bo Porter - The Stacey and Bo Porter SELF Foundation
- David Price - Project One Four
- Albert Pujols - Pujols Family Foundation
- C.C. Sabathia - PitCCh In Foundation
- Johan Santana - Johan Santana Foundation
- Chase Utley - The Utley Foundation
- Shane Victorino - Shane Victorino Foundation
- Josh Willingham - Josh Willingham Foundation
- C.J. Wilson - C.J. Wilson's Children's Charities
- David Wright - David Wright Foundation
- Kevin Youkilis - Youk's Kids
- Ryan Zimmerman - zIMS Foundation
- Ernie Banks - Ernie Banks Live Above and Beyond Foundation
- Gary Carter - The Gary Carter Foundation
- Johnny Damon - The Johnny Damon Foundation
- Matt Diaz - Diaz Family Foundation
- Tony Gwynn - The Tony & Alicia Gwynn Foundation
- Orlando Hudson - C.A.T.C.H. Foundation
- Bo Jackson - Bo Jackson's Give Me A Chance Foundation
- Fergie Jenkins - The Fergie Jenkins Foundation
- Chipper Jones - Chipper Jones Family Foundation
- Tony LaRussa - Tony LaRussa's Animal Rescue Foundation
- Cory Lidle - Cory Lidle Foundation
- Tug McGraw - The Tug McGraw Foundation
- Jamie Moyer - The Moyer Foundation
- Dale Murphy - I Won't Cheat!
- Mike Mussina - The Mike Mussina Foundation
- Joe Niekro - The Joe Niekro Foundation
- Cal Ripken, Sr. - Cal Ripken, Sr. Foundation
- Tim Salmon - Tim Salmon Foundation
- Willie Stargell - The Willie Stargell Foundation
- Darryl Strawberry - The Darryl Strawberry Foundation
- Mike Sweeney - The Mike & Shara Sweeney Foundation
- Joe Torre - Joe Torre Safe At Home Foundation
- Dave Winfield - The Winfield Foundation
- Kerry Wood - The Wood Family Foundation

BASKETBALL

- Ray Allen - Ray of Hope Foundation
- Carmelo Anthony - Carmelo Anthony Foundation
- Renaldo Balkman - Balkman Buddies Foundation
- Brandon Bass - Brandon Bass Reach Back Foundation
- Shane Battier - Battier Take Charge Foundation
- Andray Blatche - Andray Blatche Foundation
- Jim Boeheim - The Jim & Juli Boeheim Foundation
- Corey Brewer - The Corey Brewer Foundation
- Ronnie Brewer - The Ronnie Brewer Foundation
- Shannon Brown - The Shannon Brown Foundation
- Caron Butler - 3D Foundation
- John Calipari - Calipari Family Foundation
- Vince Carter - Embassy of Hope Foundation
- Mario V. Chalmers - The Mario V. Chalmers Foundation
- Glen Davis - The Glen "Big Baby" Davis Foundation
- DeMar DeRozan - The DeMar DeRozan Foundation
- Boris Diaw - Baba'Cards
- Tim Duncan - The Tim Duncan Foundation
- Kevin Durant - Kevin Durant Family Foundation
- Monta Ellis - The ME8 Foundation
- Jordan Farmar - The Jordan Farmar Foundation
- Randy Foye - Randy Foye Foundation
- Channing Frye - The Frye Family Foundation
- Manu Ginobili - Manu Ginobili Foundation
- Eric Gordon - Eric Gordon Foundation
- Marcin Gortat - MG13 Foundation
- Dwight Howard - The Dwight D. Howard Foundation
- Lebron James - The Lebron James Family Foundation
- Jason Kidd - The Jason Kidd Foundation
- Kyle Korver - The Kyle Korver Foundation
- Jeremy Lin - The Jeremy Lin Foundation
- C.J. Miles - C.J. Miles All Stars Foundation
- Steve Nash - The Steve Nash Foundation
- Joakim Noah - Noah's Arc Foundation
- Bill Self - Bill Self's Assist Foundation
- Amar'e Stoudemire - The Amar'e Stoudemire Foundation
- Jason Thompson - The Jason Thompson Foundation
- Ronny Turiaf - The Ronny Turiaf Heart to Heart Foundation

- Dwyane Wade - Wade's World Foundation
- Martell Webster - The Martell Webster Foundation
- Deron Williams - Point of Hope Foundation
- Dorrell Wright - D Wright Way Foundation
- Red Auerbach - Red Auerbach Youth Foundation
- Larry Bird - Larry Legend Foundation
- Juwan Howard - The Juwan Howard Foundation
- Magic Johnson - The Magic Johnson Foundation
- Tracy McGrady - The Tracy McGrady Foundation
- David Robinson - David Robinson Foundation
- Pat Summitt - The Pat Summitt Foundation
- Jim Valvano - The Jimmy V Foundation
- Lenny Wilkens - Lenny Wilkens Foundation
- James Worthy - James Worthy Foundation

FOOTBALL

- David Akers - Kicks for Kids
- Keenan Allen - The Keenan Allen Foundation
- Miles Austin - Austin Family Family
- Champ Bailey - Bailey Brothers Foundation
- Rob Bironas - The Rob Bironas Fund
- Dwayne Bowe - The Un-Bowe-lievable Foundation Fund
- Deion Branch - The Deion Branch Charitable Foundation
- Drew Brees - The Brees Dream Foundation
- Lance Briggs - Briggs4Kidz
- Keith Brooking - The Keith Brooking Children's Foundation
- Antonio Brown - Antonio Brown Charities
- Brent Celek - Brent Celek's Take Flight Foundation
- Desmond Clark - 88 Wayz Youth Organization
- Jay Cutler - The Jay Cutler Foundation
- Rashied Davis - Rashied Davis Charities
- Matt Elam - T.E.A.M. Elam
- Jimbo Fisher - Kidz1stFund
- Larry Fitzgerald - The First Down Fund
- Drayton Florence - The Drayton Florence Foundation
- Dwight Freeney - The Dwight Freeney Foundation
- Robbie Gould - The Goulden Touch
- Jabari Greer - The Greer Campaign
- Israel Idonije - The Israel Idonije Foundation

- Malcolm Jenkins - The Malcolm Jenkins Foundation
- Andre Johnson - Andre Johnson Charitable Foundation
- Calvin Johnson Jr. - Calvin Johnson Jr. Foundation
- Brian Kelly - Kelly Cares Foundation
- Peyton Manning - PeyBack Foundation
- Brandon Marshall - The Brandon Marshall Foundation
- Brian Moorman - Brian Moorman's PUNT Foundation
- Ben Roethlisberger - The Ben Roethlisberger Foundation
- Nick Saban - Nick's Kids Funds
- Matt Schaub - GR8 Hope Foundation
- Ndamukong Suh - The Ndamukong Suh Family Foundation
- Charles Tillman - The Cornerstone Foundation
- Michael Vick - Team Vick Foundation
- J.J. Watt - Justin J. Watt Foundation
- Lardarius Webb - The Lardarius Webb Foundation
- Charlie Weis - Hannah & Friends
- Wes Welker - Wes Welker Foundation
- DeAngelo Williams - The DeAngelo Williams Foundation
- Adrian Wilson - Adrian Wilson Foundation
- Jason Witten - Jason Witten's SCORE Foundation
- Troy Aikman - The Troy Aikman Foundation
- Mike Alstott - Mike Alstott Family Foundation
- Charlie Batch - Best of the Batch Foundation
- Jerome Bettis - The Bus Stops Here Foundation
- Josh Bidwell - Josh Bidwell Foundation
- Derrick Brooks - Derrick Brooks Charities
- Isaac Bruce - Isaac Bruce Foundation
- Mark Brunell - Brunell Family Foundation
- Eric Dickerson - The Eric Dickerson Foundation
- Donald Driver - The Donald Driver Foundation
- Tony Dungy - Dungy Family Foundation
- Warrick Dunn - Warrick Dunn Family Foundation
- Boomer Esiason - Boomer Esiason Foundation
- Doug Flutie - Doug Flutie Foundation for Autism
- Edgerrin James - Edgerrin James Foundation
- Ray Lewis - The Ray Lewis 52 Foundation
- Matt Light - The Light Foundation
- John Lynch - John Lynch Foundation
- Dan Marino - The Dan Marino Foundation

- Jonathan Ogden - The Jonathan Ogden Foundation
- Christian Okoye - The Christian Okoye Foundation
- Ara Parseghian - Ara Parseghian Medical Research Foundation
- Walter Payton - The Walter & Connie Payton Founation
- Mark Rypien - The Rypien Foundation
- Emmitt Smith - Pat & Emmitt Smith Charities
- John Stallworth - John Stallworth Foundation
- Jason Taylor - Jason Taylor Foundation
- Tim Tebow - The Tim Tebow Foundation
- Pat Tillman - The Pat Tillman Foundation
- LaDainian Tomlinson - LaDainian Tomlinson's Touching Lives Foundation
- Hines Ward - The Hines Ward's Charity
- Kurt Warner - First Things First Foundation
- Reggie White - The Reggie White Sleep Disorders Research & Education Foundation
- Steve Young - Forever Young Foundation

HOCKEY

- Marian Gaborik - The Marion Gaborik Foundation
- Tim Thomas - The Tim Thomas Foundation
- Wayne Gretzky - The Wayne Gretzky Foundation
- Mario Lemieux - The Mario Lemiuex Foundation

SOCCER

- Mario Balotelli - Mario & Charity
- Craig Bellamy - The Craig Bellamy Foundation
- Didier Drogba - The Didier Drogba Foundation
- Michael Essien - Michael Essien Foundation
- Samuel Eto'o - Fundacion Privada Samuel Eto'o
- Nwankwo Kanu - Kanu Heart Foundation
- Dirk Kuyt - The Dirk Kuyt Foundation
- Billy Sharp - Luey Jacob Sharp Foundation
- Jack Wilshere - Jack's Fund

SKATEBOARDING

- Rob Dyrdek - Rob Dyrdek Foundation

- Tony Hawk - Tony Hawk Foundation
- Ryan Sheckler - The Sheckler Foundation

RACECAR DRIVING

- Greg Biffle - The Greg Biffle Foundation
- Kurt Busch - The Kurt Busch Foundation
- Kyle Busch - The Kyle Busch Foundation
- Jeff Gordon - The Jeff Gordon Children's Foundation
- Jimmie Johnson - The Jimmie Johnson Foundation
- Ryan Newman - The Ryan Newman Foundation
- Kyle Petty - Victory Junction
- Tony Stewart - The Tony Stewart Foundation

TENNIS

- Katrina Adams - Harlem (N.Y.) Junior Tennis and Education Program
- Leslie Allen - The Leslie Allen Foundation/Win 4 Life
- James Blake - Thomas Blake Sr. Memorial Research Fund (at Sloan-Kettering)
- Todd Martin - The Todd Martin Development Fund
- Andy Roddick - The Andy Roddick Foundation
- Pam Shriver - Baltimore Community Foundation Tennis Challenge
- MaliVai Washington - MaliVai Washington Kids Foundation
- Andre Agassi - Andre Agassi Charitable Foundation
- Serena Williams - Serena Williams Fund

CHAPTER 11: THEOLOGY OF FACILITATING CHANGE | MEASURABLE IMPACT

"Transformational leadership pushes you further, strains you greater, but will ultimately give you the change you desire. Are you up for it?" --Unknown

Implementing transformational change comes with great challenges but once transformational change is accomplished, it moves mountains. One of the number one quotes used by subpar to average people is "We've always done it this way."

When transformational leadership arrives at a mediocre to below average environment, the immediate defense for the residing culture is to resent and rebuke the incoming leadership. The residing culture will work tirelessly to discredit the character and core values of the potential leader. The change needed will not happen unless a superior leader recognizes the intent surrounding the environment and boldly risks taking an unpopular stance. If need be, the superior leader must be willing to stand alone on the island of undeniable change.

This is called **Transformational Leadership** and it is not easily obtained nor sustained. If you are in a leadership position, stop, take a deep breath, look around and ask yourself, "Am I transforming the culture or am I simply making transactions?" Transactions are the equivalent to rearranging the furniture on the deck of the Titanic. Transformational leaders are willing to do whatever is necessary to create a championship environment and sustainable culture of excellence, even when it is not the popular decision! Transformational leaders are willing to go "Against All Odds."

Against All Odds

We have all had barriers of some kind in our lives, barriers that seem unfair on one hand and completely stacked odds against success on the other hand.

Our country has witnessed some historic examples of the odds being stacked against certain groups unfairly. Jackie Robinson broke the color barrier in MLB in 1947. The Tuskegee Airmen, a group of roughly one thousand black pilots that defended our country in World War II, had to teach themselves to fly. The situation was not ideal for Jackie Robinson nor for the Tuskegee Airmen, but with perseverance and determination, they defeated the odds.

> *"Life isn't about waiting for the storm to pass, it's about learning how to dance in the rain." -- Anonymous, more recently attributed to Vivian Greene*

> *"He that waits for conditions to be just right does nothing."* ECCLESIASTES 11:4

> God says, *"Love the Lord your God with all your heart and with all your soul with all your strength and with all your mind, and Love your neighbor as yourself."* LUKE 10:27

Who are our neighbors?

> *"The one who had mercy on him."* Jesus told him, *"Go and do likewise."* LUKE 10:37

The God we serve loves without any "isms" and he calls for us to love likewise.

Are there barriers between you and others that need to come down? If so, I believe reading the next section about Branch Rickey will give you some valuable insight to one of sport's most transformational leaders of all time. Branch Rickey's willingness to stand alone on an island and break the barrier changed not just baseball, but it changed America.

Branch Rickey

On the rare occasion a human being can move mountains. Most generations come and go without witnessing such a sight. But the people of the 1947 generation did see such a feat. The mountain mover came in the form of a man named Branch Rickey.

Wesley Branch Rickey was born in 1881 to a tight-knit, deeply religious Ohio family. Named after John Wesley, the founder of Methodism, Branch's upbringing was in a pious, Methodist household. The "Branch" part of his name came from the scriptures mention of a "branch" that helped make Wesley a saint. He attended school in a one-room schoolhouse in Rush Township, Ohio and later in the nearby town of Lucasville, but was unable to earn a high school diploma since the school didn't offer one. Instead, with the help from a sympathetic retired teacher, he educated himself enough to become the teacher at the local grade school, saving money for college. He taught himself Latin, higher mathematics and other subjects, and eventually was able to enter Ohio Wesleyan University. Rickey earned his way through Ohio Wesleyan by playing both baseball and football. When he realized he could make money to pay for college, he entered baseball's semipro summer circuit in 1902 and began to coach the university team the next spring.

In 1904, after graduation his contract was purchased by the Cincinnati Reds near the end of the season. He spent parts of the next three seasons in the majors, earning a reputation as a marginal catcher, a poor hitter - he couldn't hit or throw. As a catcher for the St. Louis Browns, he set a Major League record for allowing the most stolen bases in a game, 13. And because of a promise he made to his mother, Branch Rickey refused to play on Sundays.

After marrying Jane in June 1906, he had a laundry list of jobs. He was Ohio Wesleyan's athletic director, while also coaching football, basketball, and baseball. He was secretary of the Delaware, Ohio, YMCA, and he taught beginning law classes even while taking other law classes as a student.

In 1911, at nearly 30 years old, Branch Rickey graduated from law school and chose Boise, Idaho, as the site of his law office. When the trade of being an attorney did not work out for him, the impressions he had made as a baseball player and coach came to his rescue. Robert Hedges, owner of the St. Louis Browns, who had been impressed with Rickey's intelligence and articulate presentations when he was a player, offered him the job of front office executive in 1913. Rickey became the team's manager for the final 12 games of the season, and managed the team for two more full seasons.

Once his stint with the Browns was up, he began a 25-year association with the St. Louis Cardinals—first as president (1916-1919), then as field manager (1919-25), and finally taking on the general manager role (1925-1942). After serving in the U.S. Army as an officer in the Chemical Warfare Service, Branch returned to the Cardinals in 1918. Mr. Rickey assumed the field management and started the "farm" idea. It had its origin in 1919, when the Cardinals bought an 18 per cent interest in the Houston club of the Texas League. Pulitzer Prize-winning journalist Jimmy Breslin writes that Rickey was a businessman, and his genius lay in developing the best talent for the least money. He invented the farm system, which says Breslin, "...gathered players of promise and grew them, like crops, on minor league teams...". (Breslin, 2012) Farm clubs not only helped the Cardinals, they also made Rickey a rich man. With so much talent on hand, he sold players to other organizations at a personal commission of 10%.

In his years with the Cardinals, Rickey made his club recurring contenders in the National League with his astute negotiating tactics. He was known as the "master trader" of his time, using shrewd judgment in the trading of many top stars, often when they had passed their peak as performers but could still draw a high price. His most famous deal was probably the sale of Dizzy Dean to the Chicago Cubs in 1937. In exchange for the pitcher who was suffering from a sore arm, he obtained the pitchers Curt Davis and Clyde Shoun and a lump sum reported to have been $185,000. During this time, he is also credited with the introduction of the batting helmet.

Branch Rickey left the Cardinals in 1942 to join the Brooklyn Dodgers as president of the club. It was during this time that Branch Rickey really started hitting his stride. According to Rickey, "the fire in him to fix a nation began in 1904 on the practice fields at Ohio Wesleyan University", (Breslin, 2012) where he, as a student coach, first saw Charlie Thomas play baseball. As a black man, Thomas was denied access to a hotel before a game against the University of Notre Dame. Enraged, Rickey took the player to his room, ordered a cot to be sent up and made it clear that the team stayed together or left together. They stayed. But as Thomas sat in Rickey's room he began to cry and tried to rub off his skin color saying, "Black skin, black skin. If only I could rub it off and make it white." Rickey replied to the hurting player, "Stop it. If you can't beat this, how do you expect me to?" And so his journey to right America's wrong began. Rickey, writes Breslin, was "a lone white man with a fierce belief that it is the deepest sin against God to hold color against a person."

In the early years with the Brooklyn Dodgers, Branch Rickey devised his six-point plan to integrate baseball. (Breslin, 2012) First, get the backing of the Dodgers' owner, George V. McLauglin. In their meeting, McLaughlin thought about how many black baseball fans there might be. "If you want to do this to get a beat on the other teams and make some money, then let's do it," he told Rickey. "But if you want to do this for some social change, forget it. We want to win and make money. Don't try to bring principle into this. If this doesn't work for money, you're sunk." "The remaining five points were: (2) find the right Negro player and (3) find the right Negro person; (4) employ public relations; (5) gain support of the Negro community; and (6) gain acceptance by his teammates." (Breslin, 2012)

In Jackie Robinson, Rickey had points two and three well covered. Robinson served in the U.S. Army during World War II and came back to a nation that was still entrenched in racism. He stood up to it and readily fought it. Rickey anticipated the harsh treatment that Robinson would receive from fans and opposing players, so in their first meeting Rickey threw scenario after scenario at Jackie to impress upon him what he really needed from the first African American man to play Major League Baseball. "Mr. Rickey, do you really want a ballplayer who is afraid to fight back?", asked Robinson. "I want a ballplayer with guts enough not to fight back. You've got to win this thing with hitting and throwing and fielding ground balls. Nothing else!" answered Branch Rickey. Robinson, for Rickey, agreed to always turn the other cheek, for three years, anyway. He knew, as did Rickey, that it was bigger than just the two of them and the Dodgers.

In August of 1945 Rickey signed Negro League star Jackie Robinson to a Minor League contract for a signing bonus of $3,500 and a salary of $600 a month, and paved the way for Robinson's Major League debut on April 15, 1947. In spite of having to fight all the other Major League team owners, and struggle with the press, he found ways to get the black community on their side.

Robinson went on to have an exceptional 10-year baseball career. He was the recipient of the inaugural MLB Rookie of the Year Award in 1947, was an All-Star for six consecutive seasons from 1949 through 1954, and won the National League Most Valuable Player Award in 1949—the first black player honored. The Dodgers won six pennants in Robinson's 10 seasons and he played in six World Series with a win 1955. In 1997, MLB "universally" retired his uniform number, 42, across all Major League teams; he was the first pro athlete in any sport to be honored in this way. MLB also adopted a new annual tradition, "Jackie Robinson Day", for the first time on April 15, 2004, on which every player on every team wears No. 42.

Jackie Robinson is remembered as the man who broke the color barrier in Major League Baseball and in 1962 he was the first African American inducted into the Baseball Hall of Fame.

Robinson's success led other owners to seek talented black players, and by 1952, there were 150 black players in organized baseball. The last of the Negro Leagues disbanded soon after this as their marquee players had all been brought into the desegregated Major Leagues.

Branch Rickey was officially deemed the leader of the desegregation in baseball revolution, and his vocal support of civil rights extended beyond the baseball field for the rest of his life. He was inducted into the Baseball Hall of Fame in 1967. He died at the age of 83.

In addition to his fight for civil rights on and off the field, Branch Rickey was a firm proponent of the need for his players to complete their education. He once wrote to the father of a prospective ballplayer encouraging him to have his son finish college. He wrote of the man's son, "An educated ballplayer is the best. Stay with your education. You can try baseball for a while and then you'll have the college helping you the rest of your life."

So Branch Rickey was indeed a mover of mountains that profoundly changed the game – most notably his development of the farm system and breaking the color barrier. But he was also a model of how to use one's life to serve the good of others and leave a legacy. He is known to have said, "It is not the honor you take with you, but the heritage you leave behind."

And that, friends, is "The End Game".

CHAPTER 12: SUSTAINABLE PERSPECTIVES | SPORTS LEGACY PhD

"What you do for yourself will die with you, what you do for others will live forever." --Bo Porter

When I think about words like *sustainable* and *PhD* as it relates to impacting, mentoring and influencing others, the word legacy is the first word that comes to mind. A legacy can be hard to define at times because the person who truly understands the essence of serving is not keeping score or looking for any awards. These are special people who are deeply grounded in faith and understand their "why". They are willing to answer the call at every level and are honored to be the bridge for those willing to cross.

As I look back on my life, there were many people who played major roles in my overall development. But there was one man who came into my life during my most formidable years and provided me with four distinct life perspectives after which I now model my life.

This great man was the ideal influence in my life by serving as a positive role model. His Inspiration was motivating because he provided meaning and challenges. He intellectually stimulated me with creative and innovative questions about life, which piqued my interested and caused me to ask even more questions. Those questions led to him providing meaningful answers and solutions. Last but surely not the least, this man showed individualized consideration by paying special attention to my every need and concerns; he was my mentor, coach and father figure at a time when I needed it most.

This man was my Coach Bill Hicks!

If ever a man contributed to his community on every level, it was Bill Hicks. He had a positive impact on thousands of youngsters through his exceptional leadership skills. Bill believed in strict discipline and instilled a "practice makes perfect" attitude. He often took his teams out of state to introduce them to life beyond their neighborhoods. As coach of the Project Pride Little League All-Stars, he took his team on an impactful trip to Puerto Rico. After retiring from the Newark Police Department, where he also worked as a division detective, he moved to Fort Pierce,

Florida and continued inspiring youth as the Head Coach of the town's Little League teams and Head Coach at the local high school. Bill was a victim's advocate with the Fort Pierce Police Department, a police chaplain, and an ordained minister.

Sadly, on December 13, 2015 the world lost Bill Hicks and I lost my mentor, father figure and friend. As a tribute to my beloved Coach Hicks upon his death, my family wrote and published this letter in the local New Jersey newspaper. We can never really express the profound impact Bill Hicks had on our lives, but we hope our sentiments will in a small way convey our deep love and respect for him.

To Our Dearly Departed Friend,

Bill Hicks was a special part of our lives as an athletic advisor, a law enforcement officer, and most importantly, a friend. While the original reason we came to know him was through sports, he soon became entrenched in our daily activities as a de facto member of the Porter family. Coach Hicks, as we lovingly and reverently referred to him, was originally an individual only interested in the athletic potential of "Mark", as he always called Bo; yet he provided us so much more. He was a father figure to us all; a shining example of taking a genuine interest in and responsibility for the growth of other people. Coach Hicks could be called upon in any situation and was never too busy to help any of us, regardless of circumstances, in any manner possible.

Beyond all Coach Hicks provided us individually and collectively, he also leaves behind a legacy in the city of Newark for his servitude and community involvement. He fought to see fairness and justice, which he accomplished using of kindness, humanity, and intellect. He was committed to excellence and positivity. His goal was always to bring out the absolute best in everyone with whom he had the opportunity to interact. Coach Hicks could see potential in people and was often able to instill a sense of hope in those whose lives he touched. He taught so many people to be responsible for ensuring a positive, sustainable future. He wanted everyone to be a responsible citizen and respected member of their community. He led by example.

The passion with which Coach Hicks used to enrich our lives and the lives of countless others will be his legacy. His life is blueprint to us all of what it truly means to be fully committed to growing a community filled with excellence, wherever you are in the world.

While we often did so privately and regularly, today we publicly salute you "Coach" Bill Hicks. The many life lessons and experiences you

have shared with our family will never be forgotten. Thank you for sharing your light with us all. We will always love and cherish the memories you have provided. Rest well with our Heavenly Father, dear friend.
With highest regard,
The Porter Family

Bill Hicks really did it all with heart, commitment and dedication. Coach, I love you with all my heart! Rest in peace and I will continue your legacy by paying forward the blessing God gave me with you!

As a result of the impact Bill Hicks had on me, I created a student-athlete scholarship at my high school alma mater, Weequahic High School. Marvin Kennedy was one of the first recipients of this award. Some years later I received this message on Facebook from Marvin:

Marvin Kennedy: Over twenty years ago you presented me with the Marquis "Bo" Porter Student-Athlete award after a Weequahic HS football game in person. I don't think I ever got a chance to truly thank you. That day you simply changed my life. You gave what I needed to leave Newark and attend Western Connecticut State University. Thank you for inspiring me and continuing to do so...
- "So hard to be a Weequahic Indian"

Bo Porter: Marvin, it was my pleasure! I want to congratulate you for carrying the torch forward. We can do for others but they must be willing to do their part as well. I'm honored to have motivated you and pray that you can do the same for someone else someday. Praying for continued blessings and success! #IndianPride

A Little Boy Meets His Role Model

Let's face what I believe to be a fact: athletes are role models and they can have an everlasting impact on a person's life, especially young children. I am a living example of the impact an athlete can have on a person without even knowing. You have already read about how the community service of Mr. Taylor enabled me to participate in Little League baseball. Well, that was only the beginning of what God had in store for my life.

It was the summer of 1982 and my Little League coach Mr. Miller received free tickets to a New York Yankees game. Mr. Miller used the tickets to take his entire Little League team to the game. We arrived early enough to watch batting practice and we were blessed to meet New York

Yankees superstar Dave Winfield. Sitting there in complete and total shock of what was happening around me, I remember Dave talking to the group of young baseball players and signing autographs. After getting Dave's autograph we headed to our seats in right field.

Here I was, a kid from Newark, NJ attending my first Major League Baseball game at Yankee Stadium. What happened next is why all athletes should embrace the responsibility of being a role model. As I sat in my seat watching the game, something came over me. I felt and thought things that I had never before experienced. My mind started racing and it was like everything around me stopped. All I could see was the vision that one day I would be playing on this very field and signing autographs for kids. My image of success became crystal clear - so clear that it impacted every other sector of my life, from my daily behavior to an even more focused commitment to my academics and desire to work every day to improve my overall skills.

Here is what is so amazing about being a servant and vessel for God's Kingdom: Dave Winfield didn't know who I was when he signed my ball that summer day in June 1982. Fast forward 34 years to October 2016 and Dave Winfield and I share a brotherly bond that started out as an athlete honoring his responsibility to promote the game and inspire children and now has grown into a story that jump-started the life's work of a kid from Newark to accomplish real excellence.

What I have learned in life through sports is that your gifts are not about you, your leadership is not about you, your purpose is not about you. A life of significance is about serving those who need your gifts, your leadership and your purpose. The man who signifies those qualities and has earned his PhD in Sports Legacy is Dave Winfield, The SELF Foundation 2015 Torch Award Recipient and philanthropic trailblazer for athletes.

> *"You never know --what you say or do-- how it's going to affect someone else but to hear it from someone who has done well and will continue to do great things, it's fantastic. That's a life worthwhile, a career worthwhile, when you are affecting someone else in a positive way that's the way you pass it on, pass it forward." --Dave Winfield*

Dave Winfield - The Philanthropic Trailblazer For Professional Athletes

It can be no coincidence that Dave Winfield was born on October 3,

1951… the same day Bobby Thomson hit his pennant-winning home run for the New York Giants, known as "the shot heard 'round the world". With that kind of baseball karma surrounding one's birth, Dave Winfield's baseball greatness was already a given from Day 1! But baseball greatness aside, there is so much more depth to him than 3,110 career hits, 465 home runs, 1,833 RBI, 2,973 games played, 12 consecutive All-Star games, 7 Gold Gloves, 6 Silver Slugger Awards and induction into the National Baseball Hall of Fame in his first year of eligibility.

Raised in St. Paul, MN, Dave honed his athletic skills on the Oxford playground, a half block from his childhood home. He played for six Major League teams during his 22-year baseball career, but the uniform he was most proud to wear read "Oxford" across the chest. To him, the uniform represented family, community and sense of purpose. "We lived half a block away, and I just remember walking down the street with them on," Winfield says. "White with stripes, or powder blue as we continued on, and that's an incredible feeling for a kid. You're part of a group that has a mission and goals. It was a lot of fun."

After high school Winfield took his athletic skills to the University of Minnesota, where he played Big Ten basketball and baseball. As an All-American in baseball, he was voted MVP of the 1973 College World Series as a pitcher. After the season, Winfield was drafted by four teams in four different leagues in three different sports. The San Diego Padres made him first round, fourth pick of the amateur draft. The Atlanta Hawks picked him in the fifth round of the National Basketball Association draft, the Utah Stars drafted him in the fourth round of the American Basketball Association draft, and—even though he never played high-school or college football—the Minnesota Vikings selected Winfield in the seventeenth round of the National Football League draft. He chose to go down the baseball career path but never spent a day in the Minor Leagues. He went straight to the Major Leagues. Even today, he remains the only athlete ever to be drafted in by four professional sport leagues.

And so in 1973 at 21 years old, Dave Winfield took off on his professional baseball career with the San Diego Padres, followed by eight All-Star seasons with the New York Yankees. In 1990, he joined the California Angels, followed by a magical year with the Toronto Blue Jays where he drove in the winning run of the 1992 World Series. Dave returned to his native Minnesota and reached the 3,000th hit milestone with the Twins. He ended his 22-year career after the 1995 season with the American League Champion Cleveland Indians. In 2001 he was inducted into the National Baseball Hall of Fame in his first year of eligibility.

While many would take retirement from professional sports as a time to slow down and improve their golf game, Dave Winfield geared up for a new phase of his already award-winning life. In 1996, Winfield joined Fox as studio analyst for its Saturday MLB coverage. From 2001 to 2013, Winfield served as executive vice president/senior advisor of the San Diego Padres. In 2006, Winfield teamed up with conductor Bob Thompson to create The Baseball Music Project, a series of concerts that celebrate the history of baseball, with Winfield serving as host and narrator. In 2008 Winfield conceived the idea of a special draft of the surviving Negro League players to acknowledge and rectify their exclusion from the Major Leagues on the basis of race. Each Major League team drafted one player from the Negro Leagues. In 2009, Winfield joined ESPN as an analyst on its "Baseball Tonight" program. 2013 saw Winfield named special assistant to Executive Director Tony Clark at the Major League Baseball Players Association. In March 2016, Winfield helped represent Major League Baseball in Cuba during President Obama's trip to the island in an attempt to help normalize relations.

Outside of his professional baseball participation days, Dave Winfield has always been active in philanthropic work. From the beginning of his professional athletic career, Winfield began giving back to the communities in which he played. In 1973, his first year with the Padres, he began buying blocks of tickets to Padres games for families who couldn't afford to go to games, in a program known as "Pavilions." Winfield then added health clinics to the game day experience by partnering with San Diego's Scripps Clinic to have a mobile clinic brought into the stadium parking lot. When Winfield joined the Toronto Blue Jays, he learned teammate David Wells was one of the "Winfield kids" who attended Padres games. In his hometown of St. Paul, he began a scholarship program that continues to this day.

In 1977, he organized his philanthropic efforts into an official 501(c)(3) charitable organization, known as the David M. Winfield Foundation for Underprivileged Youth. Groundbreaking, Winfield was the first active athlete to establish a charitable foundation. As his salary increased, his foundation programs expanded to include holiday dinner giveaways and national scholarships. In 1978, San Diego hosted the All-

Star game, and Winfield bought his usual block of pavilion tickets. Winfield then went on a local radio station and inadvertently invited "all the kids of San Diego" to attend. To accommodate the unexpected crowd, the foundation brought the kids into batting practice. The All-Star open-practice has since been adopted by Major League Baseball and continues to date.

As a New York Yankee, he set aside $3 million of his contract for the Winfield Foundation. He funded The Dave Winfield Nutrition Center at Hackensack University Medical Center near his Teaneck, New Jersey home. The Foundation also partnered with Merck Pharmaceuticals and created an internationally acclaimed bilingual substance abuse prevention program called "Turn it Around".

Winfield's philanthropic endeavors had influence on many of MLB's players. Derek Jeter, who grew up idolizing Winfield for both his athleticism and humanitarianism, credits Winfield as the inspiration for his own Turn 2 Foundation. Of his relationship with and influence upon Derek Jeter, Winfield has said, "My visibility and play with the Yankees in the 1980's influenced him from afar. I then met him in Rookie Career Development seminar, then I met his family at Yankee events, and we all became close. You live your life and you never know whom you influence (good or bad). I'm just happy and honored to have helped make a difference in the life of someone like Derek, who played the game of baseball right, but more importantly is a positive role model to so many others." Winfield continues to help raise funds and awareness for Jeter's Foundation. In addition to influencing other MLB players to adopt the role of community steward, Winfield's work has been a precursor to today's MLB and MLB Players Association charitable components.

Recently in speaking about the history of his David M. Winfield Foundation, he said, "I no longer have my own non-profit operating foundation. I ran the Winfield Foundation for 22 years. We focused on sports, health and education, the three things that helped me succeed in life. Most of this activity was in and around the cities I played baseball in. I taught many others to carry the torch after me as I spent more and more time raising my own kids. I now do much to help others succeed in their charitable efforts." Today he has refocused his efforts towards assisting other organizations reach their business and charitable goals, in the capacity of a keynote speaker and celebrity attraction and fundraiser. He helps organizations and other foundations raise millions of dollars, gain increased visibility and an expanded base of support.

Dave Winfield is also an accomplished author and is a prolific reader of fiction and nonfiction. His autobiography, *Winfield: A Player's Life* was a New York Times best seller. Additionally, he also has written an acclaimed "how-to" called *The Complete Baseball Player*, a compilation of syndicated children's advice column called, "Ask Dave". His latest, *Dropping The Ball*, is an in-depth look at baseball's current problems and possible solutions in which he outlines his plan of action to revitalize baseball. He is a frequent contributor to the New York Times and the Los Angeles Times and has been a contributing author for NCAA.org and ThePlayersTribune.com along with the Saint Paul Pioneer Press.

If professional athlete, philanthropist, author, and baseball analyst were not enough to keep Dave Winfield busy, he also lends his talents as businessman and executive, advisor, advocate and professional speaker with an office in New York and Los Angeles. He is one of the most respected and versatile motivational speakers in the country. He addresses audiences from colleges to corporations such as American Express, MasterCard, Monster.com, Xerox, IBM, GE Small Business Solutions, General Motors, Bank of America and the FDIC. His presentations cover a wide range of topics including: It's a Game, a Science and Your Business: Your Winning Game Plan; Live a Hall of Fame Life: Your Own Pathway to Promise; The 5 Levels: From Aspiration to Achievement; and Dave Winfield: WIN in any FIELD and Do it with Character.

Those who know Dave Winfield describe him not only as one of the greatest multi-sport athletes but also as a man with integrity, credibility, and a unique ability to positively imprint and impact others. From Hall of Fame Padre/Yankee/Angel/Blue Jay/Twin/Indian to analyst/philanthropist/public speaker, it is no wonder that Dave Winfield has his own brand...literally!

Dave Winfield – 2015 SELF Foundation Torch Award Honoree had this to say about Bo Porter:

> *"Bo Porter has done some fantastic work over many years...a complete, fulfilled life is really about passing the torch of service to others over to the next generation...Kudos to Bo Porter for the great work he's doing in Houston and around the country. I'm a big fan of his now much more than even ever before." --Dave Winfield, MLB Hall of Fame Class of 2001*

The REward of Mastering The End Game

RESEARCH AND RESOLUTION

Dave Winfield, Dikembe Mutombo, Drew Brees, Peyton Manning, Tom Brady, Brett Favre, Derek Jeter, Albert Pujols, Serena Williams, Clayton Kershaw, Michael Jordon, LeBron James, Bill Parcells, Tony Dungy, Frank Robinson, Jackie Robinson, Hayden Fry, Davey Johnson, Sandy Alomar Sr., Dave Trembley. Admirable, laudable, palmary, meritorious, august, principled, estimable. One starts to run out of adjectives when describing these well-known athletes. These are a few examples of athletes who have gained the respect of others through not only their work in their respective sports, but more importantly through their work using their platform as a well-known figure to leave a legacy and impact others.

Athletes are often thought of as role models - one whose behavior, example, or success is or can be emulated by others, especially younger people. Back in 1993 Charles Barkley rejected that notion. He emphatically believed that an athlete's ability to hit home runs, score touchdowns or hit three-pointer baskets has nothing to do with being a role model. That is, having sporting ability doesn't automatically qualify a person to be a role model. Rather, he believed that is a job for parents.

But like it or not, our society has a strong dependence on athletes as role models for children and adolescents and yes, even adults. Athletes are role models whether or not they choose to take on the responsibility, and whether they are positive or negative role models.

So what qualities make an athlete a positive role model? According to Marilyn Price-Mitchell, PhD the following attributes make for a positive role model: (Price-Mitchell, 2015)

- **Passion and Ability to Inspire**
  Role models show passion for their work and have the capacity to infect others with their passion. They are authoritative and responsible with the capacity to challenge status quo as well as be diplomatic.
- **Clear Set of Values**
  Role models live their values in the world. They act in ways that support their beliefs. Role models help people understand the underlying values that motivate others to become advocates for social change and innovation. They have a track record of honesty and fair treatment of others.

- **Commitment to Community**
  Role models are *other-focused* as opposed to *self-focused*. They are usually active in their communities, freely giving of their time and talents to benefit people. Role models prioritize relationships and make time for them.
- **Selflessness and Acceptance of Others**
  Role models are selfless and accepting of others who are different from themselves. They are proactive and visible advocates for inclusion and change.
- **Ability to Overcome Obstacles**
  Role models develop the skills and abilities of initiative when they learn to overcome obstacles. They are tenacious, persistent and can withstand pressure. And they have the capacity to work with challenging situations and people.

Sports provide athletes with a platform to do tremendous good. The fact that athletes are seen as role models means they have the perfect forum in which to maximize their platform and path to leave a meaningful legacy. The question is "What will you do with it?"

Athletic careers are for the most part short lived. The question that should be foremost in each athlete's mind is, "What am I going to do to give back to the game that has given me so much? And in doing so how will this also give back to my community, my country, the world as a whole?" With proper planning, mentoring, and forethought athletes can formulate and design from early on in their sports career a plan to impact others and leave a meaningful legacy.

Leaving a legacy is not about how much money you give to charities or possessions you buy and give others. Legacy is about how one chooses to serve others. Dr. Nate Hearne (Hearne) talks about achievement versus success. He says achievement is attained when a person accomplishes great things on their own. Running backs rush for 1,500 yards, quarterbacks pass for 3,000 yards, and wide receivers have 1,800 yards of receptions in a season. These are all individual accomplishments achieved. Success is gained when a person empowers others to accomplish great things together with them. Such is the case with a coach who takes a team of athletes with varying abilities and transforms them into a championship team. But a person who leaves a deep, positive, long lasting legacy is one who empowers others to accomplish great things without him/her.

As stated earlier, with proper planning and guidance an athlete can plan early in their career to take steps to leave a great legacy. Jim Rohn was an American entrepreneur, author and motivational speaker. One of his great works was on the topic of how you leave a legacy. (Rohn, 2014) Here are the principles he says we must commit to in order to leave the legacy we desire:

- **Life is best lived in service to others.**
  This doesn't mean that we do not strive for the best for ourselves. It does mean that in all things we serve other people, including our family, co-workers and friends.
- **Consider others' interests as important as your own.**
  Much of the world suffers simply because people consider only their own interests. People are looking out for number one, but the way to leave a legacy is to also look out for others.
- **Love your neighbor even if you don't like him.**
  Liking people has to do with *emotions*. Loving people has to do with *actions*. And what you will find is that when you love them and do good by them, you will more often than not begin to like them.
- **Maintain integrity at all costs.**
  There are very few things you take to the grave with you. The number one thing is your reputation and good name. When people remember you, you want them to think, "She was the most honest person I knew. What integrity." There are always going to be temptations to cut corners and break your integrity. Do not do it. Do what is right all of the time, no matter what the cost.
- **You must risk in order to gain.**
  In just about every area of life you must risk in order to gain the reward. When we risk, we gain. And when we gain, we have more to leave for others.
- **You reap what you sow.**
  In fact, you always reap more than you sow—you plant a seed and reap a bushel. What you give you get. What you put into the ground then grows out of the ground. If you give love you will receive love. If you give time, you will gain time. It is one of the truest laws of the universe. Decide what you want out of life and then begin to sow it.
- **Hard work is never a waste.**
  No one will say, "It is too bad he was such a good, hard worker." But if you aren't they will surely say, "It's too bad he was so

lazy—he could have been so much more!" Hard work will leave a grand legacy. Give it your all on your trip around the earth. You will do a lot of good and leave a terrific legacy.

- **Don't give up when you fail.**
  Imagine what legacies would have never existed if someone had given up. How many thriving businesses would have been shut down if they quit at their first failure? Everyone fails. It is a fact of life. But those who succeed are those who do not give up when they fail. They keep going and build a successful life—and a legacy.

- **Don't ever stop in your pursuit of a legacy.**
  Many people have accomplished tremendous things later on in life. There is never a time to stop in your pursuit of a legacy. Sometimes older people will say, "I am 65. I'll never change." That won't build a great life! No, there is always time to do more and achieve more, to help more and serve more, to teach more and to learn more. Keep going and growing that legacy!

Rosa Parks said, "Each person must live their life as a model for others." In other words, use the life you have been given to not only live and fulfill your own dreams but also along the way be an example for others. The beauty of leaving a legacy is that each and every person ever born has the potential to leave the space they took up in the universe a better place than when they arrived.

So if you think about it, "The End Game is really the beginning!"

CONCLUSION

"A life is not important except in the impact it has on other lives." -- Jackie Robinson

We are living in a generation where entitlement is a popular thought of many. It is that train of thought that prohibits others from doing for others. If your core belief is that the game or life owes you something, then your passion and desire to do for others will be clouded with thoughts of "What's in it for me?" So let's set the record straight! The sports game does not owe anyone anything. If anything we owe the game. The game has given so much to so many! It is probably one of the biggest mistakes one can make - thinking the game owes them something. When you feel indebted, that sparks a desire to repay! So it is extremely important to get the thought process correct in your heart and soul. You are indebted to the game that has no ending. Pay your debt and allow the process to continue with the legacy you will leave.

One of my closest friends and mentors is Dave Trembley, a former educator, Major League Manager for the Baltimore Orioles, and true baseball lifer. Dave was my manager for two years in the Chicago Cubs Minor League System and he is famous for saying, "Respect the game and appreciate what you have, because there are countless people who have paid a heavy price for you to enjoy the opportunity you have today and there are millions of people who would trade places with you if given the chance. So don't ask what can the game do for you, ask what can you do for the game." Dave, I will never forget those words. Thank you for your wisdom, mentorship and friendship. You helped inspire me to appreciate the opportunities sports have provided and embedded a never ending desire to pay forward the one debt that I never wish nor believe I can ever pay off in full! Sports were the bridge God provided to embark His earthly plan for my life and I'm honored and humbled to have embraced God's calling on my life.

I have received numerous awards and achievements throughout my life but there is no greater earthly achievement than having someone else speak to the impact you've had on their life, as I just did about Dave Trembley. The beauty of it all is that Dave never asked or expected anything in return because Dave understands his assignment is greater than any earthly payment he could ever receive. We are all vessels being used by God and our debt is not a monetary payment. It is an understanding of why He chose us and our desire to use the platform He blessed us with to impact and empower others.

I've been asked, "Why do you give so much?" My answer has always been, "I give not because I have so much, I give because I know what it feels like to have nothing." I know where I came from and I feel truly blessed and forever grateful to be where I am today. And I know it would not have happened without the grace of God. Because I've embraced my past, I have faith that:

> *The will of God will never take me,*
> *Where the grace of God cannot keep me.*
> *Where the arms of God cannot support me,*
> *Where the riches of God cannot supply my needs,*
> *Where the power of God cannot endow me.*
>
> *--Unknown*

I understand my full assignment is to continue running the bases, hitting grand slams and paying forward one of the most fundamental character traits I learned in my Development Level of sports: be a good teammate and care about others. Throughout this book you have read numerous personal testimonies and quotes from people with whom I've shared space. I'm completely honored and humbled to have left that type of impression in their lives. Inspiring, empowering and impacting the lives of others is like hitting a grand slam and bringing everyone home safely. It brings joy to my heart that I'm not arriving safely at home plate solo. The following testimony letter from one of my former players and mentee John Duncan further speaks to being a good steward of God's game plan to continue the game that has no ENDING...

Testimony by John Duncan

My involvement with Bo Porter's programs began when I was 12 years old. I am now 26 years old and still regularly draw on the experiences and lessons that I learned through Bo's structured curriculum. I think the best way for me to explain the impact that Bo and his management team have had on my life is to share my experience.

When I first started working with Bo and his baseball staff, I was an unorganized and distracted teenager. My grades were not good. I had a C average and had very little interest in school. Over the next few years, I not only developed a high level of skill on the baseball diamond, but I also began to fill the gaps that were holding me back from achieving success in other areas. Bo holds classroom sessions each week where he teaches the importance of communication skills and having the right attitude. Bo also requires his players to create challenging goals and he monitors the progress of each player towards those goals until they are realized.

My long term goal was to get into the University of Texas. Bo pushed me to work hard and commit to this goal. By the time I graduated high school, I had all A's on my report card and got into UT. Once I was at UT, I sat down with Bo and made a new goal. I wanted to be in the McCombs Business School. Using the same strategies and mindset that I developed in Bo's courses, I was able to achieve this goal. Upon, graduation, much to my surprise, I received a phone call from Bo and he asked, "What's next?" I remember kind of laughing and thinking, "Aren't I done with this goal thing?" What I have come to find out is that you are really never done with Bo's programs and will use his lessons for the rest of your life. Bo and his staff are invested in your continuous success and will always be there to lean on. So we sat down again…. I told Bo that I wanted to work at one of the top 10 fortune 500 companies because they are known for the best finance training programs. Over the next few weeks, Bo and I worked together to build my interview skills and worked to position me to perform in front of a panel of executives. After several long interviews, I was hired into the General Electric Financial Leadership Program, where I work today as a financial analyst.

Looking back, it was really important for me to know that someone had confidence in me and took the time to continuously push me towards my goals. Bo and his staff are committed to developing responsible student-athletes with vision, drive, and confidence. They are experts at teaching the necessities to succeed in all aspects of life. The skills that you will learn through Bo's programs are truly invaluable.

The REal Scoreboard

God's scoreboard is different from ours. He judges not by money, statistics, or fame, but by the state of our hearts and desire to serve Him. God calls us to be faithful, not "successful." He calls us to follow the dreams He has put in our hearts.

> *"My thoughts are nothing like your thoughts," says the Lord.*
> *"And my ways are far beyond anything you could imagine.*
> *For just as the heavens are higher than the earth, so my ways*
> *are higher than your ways and my thoughts higher than your*
> *thoughts." ISAIAH 55: 8-9*

Trust God to bear fruit in our lives however He chooses to. Don't sell yourself or your dreams short. Be persistent in accomplishing whatever He has placed in our heart. Our diligence, persistence, and commitment to His purposes are the keys that define real excellence.

The only thing that is really important is that His purposes are accomplished. He wants hearts to change - including ours - and lives to be impacted, even when those results aren't visible to anyone. His work is done deep inside. Our job is to be faithful; His job is to accomplish results.

Are you mastering the REal GAME? If so, God bless you for answering your call. If not, let *The End Game* be your invitation to join the best game you will ever play and be a part of the greatest team this world has ever witnessed. You will be victorious on the REal Scoreboard and your END GAME will never END...

> *"The game is never over. No matter what the scoreboard*
> *reads, or what the referee says, it doesn't end when you come*
> *off the court." –Pat Summitt*

> *"Life's most persistent and urgent question is, 'What are you*
> *doing for others?' " --Martin Luther King*

REFERENCES

U.S. Census 2000. (2000). Retrieved from
http://www.census.gov/main/www/cen2000.html

(1981). *Sports Illustrated , 19*(2), p. 108.

Aspen Institute. (2015). Physical Literacy in the United States. A Model, Strategic Plan, and Call to Action. *Sports & Society Program with support from the Robert Wood Johnson Foundation.* Washington D.C: Aspen Institute.

Barron, J. M., Ewing, B. T., & Waddell, G. R. (2001). The effects of high school athletic participation on education and labor market outcomes. *Rev.Econ.Stat., 82*(3), 409-421.

Beals, K. A., & Manore, M. M. (1994). The prevalence and consequences of subclinical eating disorders in female athletes. *International Journal of Sport Nutrition, 4*, 175–195.

Bensinger, G. (n.d.). Retrieved from In Depth with Graham Bensinger: http://www.grahambensinger.com

Berger, B. G. (1991). "*The Personal and Social Benefits of Sport and Physical Activity*". *Benefits of Leisure.* (B. P. Driver, Ed.) PA: Venture Publishing Inc. .

Boys & Girls Clubs of America. . (n.d.). *Our mission.* Retrieved from http://www.bgca.org/whoweare/Pages/WhoWeAre.aspx.

Breslin, J. (2012). *Branch Rickey: A life.* New York: : Penguin Group.

Brown, B. (n.d.). Retrieved from http://www.proactivecoaching.info/proactive/

Canadian Sport For Life. (n.d.). Retrieved from http://canadiansportforlife.ca/learn-about-canadian-sport-life/ltad-stages

Carnevale, A., Strohl, J., & Melton, M. (n.d.). *What's It Worth? The Economic Value Of College Majors. 1st ed.* Retrieved Sept 13, 2016, from Center on Education and the Workforce: www.cew.georgetown.edu

CDC. (2010). *The Association Between School-Based Physical Activity, Including Physical Education, and Academic Performance.* Retrieved from U.S. Department of Health and Human Services;: http://www.cdc.gov/ HealthyYouth/health_and_academics/pdf/pa-pe_paper.pdf.

Chase, C. (2013, 11 22). *The 10 most athletic presidents of all time.* Retrieved from For the Win: http://ftw.usatoday.com/2013/11/john-f-kennedy-most-athletic-presidents

Copeland, W., Wolke, D., Angold, A., & Costello, E. (2013). Adult Psychiatric Outcomes of Bullying and Being Bullied by Peers in Childhood and Adolescence. . 2013;70(4):419-426. doi:10.1001/jamapsychiatry.2013.504 . *JAMA Psychiatry, 70*(4), 419-426.

Côté, J. &.-T. (2007). Youth involvement in sport. In Crocker (Ed.), *Introduction to sport psychology: A Canadian perspective* (pp. 266-294). Toronto: Pearson Prentice Hall.

Crooks, R. (2013, Feb 22). *From Stoked to Broke: Why Are So Many Professional Athletes Going Bankrupt?* Retrieved from Mint Life: https://blog.mint.com/how-to/from-stoked-to-broke-why-are-so-many-professional-athletes-going-bankrupt-0213/?display=wide

Dewey, J. (1938). *Experience and Education.* New York: Collier.

Dungy, T., & Whitaker, N. (2011). *The One Year Uncommon Life Daily Challenge.* (C. Stream, Ed.) IL: Tyndale House.

Eccles, J. S., & Barber, B. L. (1999). Student council, volunteering, basketball or marching band: what kind of extracurricular involvement matters? *J.Adolesc.Res., 14*(1), 10-43.

Epstein-Reeves, J. (2012, Feb 21). *Six Reasons Companies Should Embrace CSR.* Retrieved from Forbes: http://www.forbes.com/sites/csr/2012/02/21/six-reasons-companies-should-embrace-csr/#47546d734c03

Ferris, E. (2004). Academic Fit of Student-Athletes: An Analysis of NCAA Division 1-A Graduation Rates. *Research in Higher Education*, 555–575.

Foyle, A., & Redick, J. J. (2015). *Winning the money game: Lessons learned from the financial fouls of pro athletes.* New York: Amistad.

Fraser-Thomas, J. L., Cote, J., & Deakin, J. (2005, Feb). Youth Sport Programs: An Avenue to Foster Positive Youth Development. *Physical Education and Sport Pedagogy, 10*(1), 19-40.

Glanville, D. (2009, Jan 12). *Badge of Honor.* Retrieved from The New York Times: http://www.nytimes.com/2009/01/13/opinion/13glanville.html

Hamilton, S. F., Hamilton, M. A., & Pittman, K. (2004). Principles for youth development. In S. F. Hamilton (Ed.), *The youth development handbook. Coming of age in American communities* (pp. 3–22). Thousand Oaks, CA: Sage.

Hearne, N. (n.d.). *Living and Leaving A Positive Legacy.* Retrieved from The Hub: http://www.gotothehub.com/living-and-leaving-a-legacy/

History Of Social Networking: How It All Began! (2016, April 1). Retrieved from 1st Web Design: http://1stwebdesigner.com/history-of-social-networking/

Holt, N. L. (2008). *Positive youth development through sport.* London: Routledge.

Larson, R. W., Hansen, D. M., & Moneta, G. (2006). Differing profiles of developmental experiences across types of organized youth activities. *Dev.Psychol., 42*(5), 849-863.

Lerner, R. M., Fisher, C. B., & Weinberg, R. A. (2000). Toward a science for and of the people: promoting civil society through the application of developmental science. *Child Development, 71*, 11–20.

Malina, R. (2012). "Movement Proficiency in Childhood: Implications for Physical Activity and Youth Sport". *Kinesiologia Slovenica,, 18*(3), 19-34.

Marsh, M. W. (1993). The effects of participation in sport during the last 2 years of high-school. *Sociology of Sport Journal, 10*, 18–43.

National Research Council and Institute of Medicine . (2002). *Community programs to promote youth development.* Washington: National Academy Press.

National Research Council and Institute of Medicine . (2002). *Community programs to promote youth development .* Washington: National Academy Press.

NCAA . (n.d.). *Academic Success Rate (ASR).* Retrieved from NCAA: www.ncaa.org/about/resources/research/academic-success-rate-asr"

Nike. (2014, April 02). *INSIDE ACCESS: CELEBRATING DEREK JETER'S LAST SEASON WITH RE2PECT.* Retrieved from Nike News: http://news.nike.com/news/inside-access-celebrating-derek-jeter-last-season-with-re2pect

NoBullying.com. (2015, 12 22). *The Effects of Peer Pressure Bullying.* Retrieved from NoBullying.com: https://nobullying.com/peer-pressure-bullying/

O'Sullivan, J. (2014). *Changing the game.* New York : Morgan James.

Peck, S. (n.d.). *The 4 Common Types of Bullying.* Retrieved from Parents.com: http://www.parents.com/kids/problems/bullying/common-types-of-bullying/

Peterson, C., & Seligman, M. (2004). *Character Strengths and Virtues: A Handbook and Classification.* New York: American Psychological Association & Oxford University Press.

Preston, C. (2013, March 25). *Five Reasons Professional Athletes Go Broke.* Retrieved from Wyatt Investment Research: http://www.wyattresearch.com/article/five-reasons-professional-athletes-go-broke/29606/

Price-Mitchell, M. (2015). *Tomorrow's Change Makers: Reclaiming the Power of Citizenship for a New Generation.* Bainbridge,, WA: Eagle Harbor,.

RH, S. (2005). *Diversity Pedagogy:Examining the Role of Culture in the Teaching-Learning Process.* (A. a. Bacon, Ed.) Boston/ London: Pearson.

Rohn, J. (2014, June 17). *Rohn: This Is How You Leave a Legacy.* Retrieved from Success: http://www.success.com/article/rohn-this-is-how-you-leave-a-legacy

Sharma, N. (2009). *Sports History.* . New Delhi: Kendra Publishing.

Sheets, R. H. (2005). *Diversity Pedagogy: Examining the Role of Culture in the Teaching-Learning Process.* Boston/London: Pearson.

Single, J. (2016, January 19). *The key to stop bullying: Popular kids.* Retrieved from http://www.cnn.com/2016/01/19/health/popular-kids-can-stop-bullying/index.html

Smith, K. (2016, March 7). *Marketing: 96 Amazing Social Media Statistics and Facts for 2016.* Retrieved from brandwatch: https://www.brandwatch.com/2016/03/96-amazing-social-media-statistics-and-facts-for-2016/

Snyder, B. (2014, Dec 10). *Magic Johnson: The Businessman Behind the Basketball Legend.* Retrieved from Entrepreneur: https://www.entrepreneur.com/article/240734

Snyder, E. E., & Spreitzer, E. (1990). High school athletic participation as related to college attendance among Black, Hispanic, and White males: a research note. *Youth and Society, 21,* 390–398.

Staff, G. (2015, May 20). *What parents can do about childhood bullying.* Retrieved October 08, 2016, from Parenting: | . Retrieved October 08, 2016, from http://www.greatschools.org/gk/articles/what-parents-can-do-about-childhood-bullying/

USADA. (2011). What Sport Means in America A Study of Sport's Role in Society. Colorado Springs:: USADA.

USADA. (2012). True Sport: What We Stand to Lose in Our Obsession to Win. Colorado Springs:.

What parents can do about childhood bullying . (2015, May 20). Retrieved Oct 08, 2016, from | Parenting. : http://www.greatschools.org/gk/articles/what-parents-can-do-about-childhood-bullying/

Whitley, R. L. (1999). Those 'dumb jocks' are at it again: a comparison of the educational performances of athletes and nonathletes in North Carolina high school from 1993 through 1996. *High School Journal, 82,* 223–233.

ABOUT THE AUTHORS

Bo Porter

Bo Porter is living proof that, if given a bridge of opportunity, anyone can reach the peak of his or her potential. He possesses fortitude, a burning desire to attain ambitious goals, and the work ethic it takes to reach and sustain success. An accomplished professional athlete, Major League Baseball (MLB) Executive, entrepreneur, business developer and philanthropist. Bo knows how to empower himself and others to attain the highest levels of personal and professional achievement.

Born and raised in the heart of inner-city Newark, New Jersey, Bo faced many obstacles and long odds of overcoming his environment and the circumstances surrounding his upbringing. His first bridge of opportunity came in the form of a kind gesture from a neighborhood friend. This one gesture opened the first of many doors that would propel Bo though a series of accomplishments that continue to this day.

Bo was drafted by the Cubs in 1993, and earned his Communications degree from the University of Iowa in 1994. He played in the Major Leagues for the Cubs, Oakland A's and Texas Rangers. He also coached for the Miami Marlins, Arizona Diamondbacks, Washington Nationals, and Atlanta Braves.

At the age of 40, the Houston Astros hired Bo as Manager, making him the youngest manager in MLB at the time. He completed the trifecta of the MLB hierarchy when he was named Special Assistant General Manager of the Atlanta Braves. He was later promoted to Director of the Major League Baseball Players Association Players Trust & Player Development. Bo transitioned into broadcast media when he was hired by the Mid-Atlantic Sports Network (MASN) as the Pre & Post Game Analyst for the World Series Champions Washington Nationals. He currently works for the MLB Commissioner's Office as the Director of Coaching Development and is a broadcast analyst for MLB Network.

Bo is a nationally acclaimed Keynote Speaker, known as "The Coach of Champions." He's the Founder and Chairman of the Board for Bo Porter Academy, Founding President of Future All-Stars Sports Development Academy, CEO of Bo Porter Enterprise, Founder and CEO of CORE Multimedia Group and the author of two books REal Life EMPOWERED and The END GAME.

Bo received Mayoral Proclamations and Keys to the City from the Mayors of both Newark, NJ and Houston, Texas. Bo received a Proclamation from Houston's Mayor Sylvester Turner on February 7, 2017, a day that was proclaimed Bo Porter Day in Houston, Texas. Bo also received a Proclamation from the Essex County Executive Joe DiVincenzo on December 13, 2012, a day that was proclaimed Bo Porter Day in Essex County, New Jersey. On May 5, 2015, Newark, New Jersey's Mayor Ras Baraka renamed Green Acres Park the Marquis "Bo" Porter Sports Complex. The mayor said, "The renaming of this park is a tribute to Bo's lifetime accomplishments and commitment to our great city." Bo was inducted into the Newark Athletic Hall of Fame in 2001. He was inducted into the Weequahic High School Alumni Association Hall of Fame in 2018.

Bo is a visionary who creates an environment that centers around positive movements and transformational growth. Bo is an entrepreneur at heart, a change agent for all that is good and a true champion. He lives in Missouri City, Texas with his wife Dr. Heather Brown and their three sons Bryce, Jaxon and Jace.

Debbi Taylor

Debbi Wrobleski Taylor grew up in Nashua, New Hampshire and covered local high school and college sports teams in addition to the Red Sox, Celtics, Bruins and Patriots. While working at the New England Sports Network she created a "Teacher of the Week" segment spotlighting influential teachers of local professional athletes. She won two Emmy Awards at NESN for hosting, writing and producing "Baseball in the Dominican Republic" and "The Friendship Games in Cuba". Debbi was only the second woman (former Red Sox owner Jean Yawkey was the first) to be recognized by Red Sox Hall of Famer Ted Williams in his Hitter's Hall of Fame. She won a National Emmy as a producer at ESPN and she worked in our nation's capital for five seasons as the in-game television reporter for the Washington Nationals Baseball Team.

Debbi is graduate of the Northfield Mount Hermon School and the University of Illinois (Champaign-Urbana). She earned her Master's Degree in Broadcast Journalism at Northwestern University's Medill School of Journalism. She lives in Central Florida with her husband Wade and daughter Kaitlyn who both share her passion for baseball. Debbi spends her free time supporting youth programs and children's charities. She will always hold a special place in her heart for the Jimmy Fund and the Dana Farber Cancer Institute in Boston. Debbi dedicates this book to her mom, Patricia Wrobleski, the woman who continues to inspire her to believe in her dreams.

Made in the USA
Middletown, DE
15 November 2025

21633025R00096